D1569471

Rae Katherine's Victorian Recipe Secrets

Rae Katherine's Victorian Recipe Secrets

BY RAE KATHERINE EIGHMEY

HOWELL PRESS

Designed by Janet Wilkins

Edited by Katherine A. Neale and Anne Montgomery

Printed in Hong Kong

Published by Howell Press, Inc., 1147 River Road, Suite 2,

Charlottesville, Virginia 22901. Telephone (804) 977-4006

First Printing

Library of Congress Cataloging-in-Publication Data

Eighmey, Rae Katherine.

Rae Katherine's Victorian Recipe Secrets / by Rae Katherine Eighmey.

p. cm.

Includes bibliographical references and index.

ISBN: 1-57427-045-1.

1. Cookery.   I. Title.

TX715.E54 1995   641.5

QB195-20434

REGARDING NUTRITIONAL INFORMATION

The nutritional analysis at the end of each recipe was performed by Micro Cookbook 1.0 published by Pinpoint Publishing of Santa Rosa, California, and is provided for guidelines only. The nutritional information is for one individual serving unless otherwise indicated. Where the ingredient lists suggest butter or margarine, the nutritional information is based on the margarine figures.

Illustrations for this book have come from 1884 and 1885 editions of *Good Housekeeping* magazine and *The New England Cookbook*, published in 1905 by Chas. E. Brown Publishing Company, Boston.

*For my mother and father and in memory of
Emma Catherine Hague, my paternal grandmother,
whose handwritten recipe cards started this exploration
into yesterday's foods*

Table of Contents

ACKNOWLEDGMENTS

any people have helped make this volume possible. My special thanks to Betsy Hayslip, executive director of the Heritage Commission of Tuscaloosa County and a good friend. Appreciation also goes to those who have helped refine the recipe adaptations and bravely tasted the many versions and variations, most especially Kay and Jerry Culton. I would also like to thank the reference librarians at the Stanley Hoole Special Collections of the University of Alabama and, in particular, Mr. Clark Center, who provided guidance as well as information. While most of the recipes came from books in my own collection, some of the works referenced here came from the main collection of the University of Alabama library, which frequently had just the volume I needed right on the shelf. Finally, special thanks are owed to Kate Neale at Howell Press. Her insightful suggestions and careful editing made a significant impact on the way the instructions in my head made it to the page.

I am indebted to all of those chefs, housekeepers, and just plain cooks who have gone before and who took the time to write down their cooking secrets. And, most importantly, I must share this with my husband, John. Without his support and prodding, this work would still be a stack of ingredient-spattered recipes in progress.

INTRODUCTION

"A surprise often captures the appetite."

Mrs. D.H.R. Goodale
Good Housekeeping, February 1885

In the spring of 1992, I had just finished transcribing the household notebook kept between 1861 and 1863 by Priscilla Taylor Jemison, wife of Robert Jemison, a Confederate statesman. Much to my frustration, there were only two recipes among the inventory of china, dress maker's orders, notations of clothing made for their household slaves, and lists of goods purchased. One of the recipes was for a type of cookie called a "jumble" and the other was for Sally Lunn, a slightly sweet yeast bread baked in a turban mold. Lists of food in the smokehouse, vegetables grown in the garden, and fruit trees planted provided some clues about the dining habits of families such as the Jemisons, but I wanted to know much more. A friend, knowing my interest, showed me two tattered cookbooks she had retrieved from a pile of old books. I began reading and cooking. Since I was already used to cooking from my grandmother's handwritten recipe cards, I knew how to translate nonstandard measurements like "teacups" and "butter the size of a walnut."

I began with those first two books and worked through scores of other books and magazines acquired in junk stores, antique shops, and libraries. I felt as though I had rediscovered an original American cuisine — one that featured a diversity of spices and herbs, a wide variety of ketchups and pickles, and the use of common foods in ways that are uncommon to us now. In these books and magazines, I discovered recipes for strawberry pickles, spaghetti baked as a dessert pie, sweet cookies with caraway seeds, and meats flavored with those aromatic spices more likely to be found today in pumpkin pie.

After researching American Victorian cooking trends and working with hundreds of recipes, I discovered four Victorian recipe secrets which changed my assumptions about American cooking during that era. These recipes are easy, healthful, economical, and different. Rather than being complicated to prepare, these recipes are simple to make. Just about anyone can re-create these dishes successfully.

Not every American Victorian housewife had a large staff. Many women, especially those living away from large urban areas, were solely responsible for cooking for their families. Several Victorian authors published housekeeping guides with recipes written for these women. Many of these recipes use techniques which are still familiar to us today even though we may use different kitchen equipment. For example, the braising of meats, which Victorian cooks did on the back of the stove, (or, earlier, in the embers of the fireplace) is easily accomplished today with a slow cooker or crock pot. The only differences are in the seasonings and cooking liquids used.

The Victorian diet was not fat laden. In fact, there was a significant health food movement during the Victorian era. Low-fat and nonfat sauces and ketchups were used much more frequently with meat and vegetable courses than cream or butter-laden toppings and high-fat gravies. Several writers, including Mrs. E.E. Kellogg and Dr. A.W. Chase, urged moderation in the consumption of meat and advocated using a variety of healthful grains and legumes in the family diet. Household guides described the role of various types of food in maintaining health and detailed the results of experiments concerning their digestibility.

This was not an era of excess. Many Victorian cookbooks admonished cooks to "use everything," and the authors wrote scores of soup, hash, croquette, bread pudding, and trifle recipes to help their readers take full advantage of meat bones, vegetable scraps, and all manner of leftovers.

While some Victorian recipes may have been influenced by the famous French, German, and English chefs of the day, there was a significant and varied *American* Victorian cuisine. Developed and promoted largely by American women food writers, this cuisine featured an abundance of ingredients found in the United States: cornmeal, molasses, turkey, cranberries, blackberries, sweet corn, and sweet potatoes are just some of the indigenous foods which gave American Victorian cuisine its unique textures and flavors.

Victorian household guides and cookbooks provided more than recipes; they included sections on the proper installation and maintenance of home improvements as well as suggestions for the proper way to run a household, including raising children, providing health care, and managing kitchen help. One bibliography lists nineteen of these books as being published in America during 1838 alone, while during 1851, 43 were published.*

By the middle of the nineteenth century, innovations in cooking equipment and the availability of new kinds of ingredients meant that it was no longer practical for women to continue cooking using the same techniques as their mothers and grandmothers. With the new wood, gas, or coal freestanding cookstove, women could control the degree of heat much more precisely. The introduction of chemical leavening agents such as baking soda and cream of tartar and, eventually, composed baking powder, enabled Victorian cooks to create an increased variety of cakes, breads, and cookies which were lighter and easier to prepare than those raised only by beaten egg whites or yeast. Homemakers adapted and created new recipes to take full advantage of these technological innovations.

In the 1850s natural ice was being transported from New England to other regions of the United States as well as to Great Britain. By the 1880s commercial production of ice assured its availability to all regions of the country year-round, while the advent of refrigerated boxcars enabled great varieties of foods to travel from region to region. After the Civil War, improved home and commercial canning processes assured safe and reliable access to fruits and vegetables throughout the year. The ability to keep food chilled, or to "put it up" safely in sealed jars, meant that housekeepers could shift their emphasis from using food before it spoiled to the planned preparation of balanced meals.

The best of the Victorian American cookbooks gave their readers insight into ways of using traditional ingredients in new and different ways. It is my hope that this volume will continue that tradition, introducing cooks to the flavors of yesterday and easy ways to prepare them.

*Wheaton, Barbara Ketcham and Patricia Kelly.
Bibliography of Culinary History. Boston: G.K. Hall & Co, 1988.

All of the recipes in this book come from my own collection of hundreds of Victorian recipes. This is a highly personal selection. I have selected those recipes which my family and friends have most enjoyed and which, I hope, will give a sense of the difference between contemporary and Victorian American cooking. However, this is not a comprehensive guide to Victorian cuisine. Neither my husband nor I hunt, so there are no game recipes. We don't care for oysters, so even though they often appeared on the Victorian table, they will not be represented here. I have included one recipe that calls for mutton, but I use beef instead. I also choose not to cook with veal or lamb.

In converting these recipes to modern use, I retained the factors critical to the flavor and texture of the dish while taking advantage of modern equipment. Victorians loved labor-saving equipment and household gadgets. Hundreds of devices for mixing and preparing foods were patented during the Victorian era. I am sure the Victorian housekeeper would have gladly used a food processor and even a microwave oven, so I see no reason not to take full advantage of them here. And even though I have used my food processor extensively, don't be concerned it you don't have one. You can certainly chop, slice, dice, and mix by hand or with other equipment.

The only items you might not own that are essential for making these recipes are a food mill, or fine sieve, and a flour sifter. I use an eight-inch sieve for sifting, straining sauces, and pressing vegetables and fruits to remove seeds and skins. Cheesecloth and lint-free cotton or linen (not terry cloth) dish towels are necessary for straining some of the mixtures.

And if you intend to store any of the pickles or relishes longer than the suggested time or differently from the recipe's instructions, consult a canning guide for the current processing requirements necessary to assure a healthful product.

I have tried to limit the amount of fat and eliminate as much of the sodium as possible in each recipe. The resulting 77 recipes in this volume are relatively easy to prepare. I have designated the difficulty of each recipe with a spoon rating. Those recipes marked with one spoon (🥄) are the simplest to prepare, while those with three spoons (🥄🥄🥄) are more difficult or tricky.

Today my cookie jar is more likely to be filled with Walnut Molasses Bars than chocolate chip cookies. Entrees such as Pilau and Victorian Chicken Salad are enjoyed at covered dish dinners whenever I take them, and my entire family has been known to eat Mrs. Jemison's Jumbles by the handful. I know these Victorian recipe secrets will capture the appetites of your family and friends, too.

Beverages and Appetizers

"Offering the best to visitors . . . can be easily combined with the easy freedom which makes the stranger feel at home; this is the perfection of hospitable entertainment."

Catherine E. Beecher and Harriet Beecher Stowe
American Woman's Home, 1869

Entertaining at home was an important part of the Victorian social structure. Whether guests came for an evening's entertainment, or a summer in the country, authors of period cookbooks and household management guides cautioned their readers not to exceed their means while entertaining. It was more important to make guests feel comfortable and at home than it was to serve them extravagant refreshments.

Throughout the Victorian era, guests at formal dinner parties might be served a small appetizer course before the soup. The importance of a well-made appetizer was described in an essay published in 1894: "The hors d'oeuvre . . . must whet the appetite, not blunt it. In its flavor must its strength lie; at once keen and subtle, it should stimulate, but not satisfy, an anchovy salad touches perfection." Many of the appetizer recipes included here have those same combinations of savory, salty, and sharp flavors. Of particular interest are the Ginger Sandwiches, Rissoles, and Potted Ham.

Cocktail parties with small finger foods as the only food are a twentieth century practice. An article in the December 1901 edition of the *Boston Cooking School Magazine* documents the increasing importance of appetizers: "The standard Italian custom — once considered so very Bohemian — of prefacing the meal with little 'kickshaws' carefully prepared and served, has obtained. In Russia these relishes or hors d'oeuvres . . . form quite a meal in themselves."

Likewise, the types of beverages a Victorian hostess served her guests shifted during the period from wine, beer, and other spirits to the moderation, or even elimination, of alcohol. By the middle of the Victorian period, the Temperance movement was in full swing.

Waging war against the evils of drink became an important responsi-bility of the homemaker. "Well- cooked, palatable meals are safeguards against the evils of the ale-house . . . Seldom is a well-fed man a drunkard," wrote the anonymous author of the *Dixie Cookbook*. Influen- tial women urged the elimi-nation of all alcoholic bever- ages. Poems and songs with titles such as, "Please Don't Sell My Father Rum" and "Lips That Touch Liquor Shall Never Touch Mine" appeared in newspapers with regularity. The Black-berry Cordial and Raspberry Shrub included here are examples of "soft" beverages popular before the age of Coca-Cola. I have also included a couple of alcoholic punch recipes that Carrie Nation would never have served.

Mrs. Cleveland's Wedding Lunch

Consommé en tasse

Soft Shell Crabs

Coquilles de Ris de Vean

Snipes on Toast

Lettuce and Tomato Salad

Fancy Ice Cream

Cakes

Tea

Coffee

Fruits

Mottos

When 49-year-old bachelor President Grover Cleveland married Frances Folsom, the 22-year-old daughter of his law partner, the White House gained a graceful hostess whom some have called our most beautiful first lady.

Zeimann, Hugo and F.L. Gillette. *The White House Cook Book*. Chicago: The Werner Company, 1899.

2

Blackberry Cordial

Cordials and shrubs are among the oldest recipes in this collection. Some recipes suggest adding 1/2 cup "good brandy" to the concentrate and drinking the beverage undiluted in small cordial glasses, but I much prefer to mix the syrup with seltzer or spring water. As the author of one period cookbook suggested, raspberry shrub is a "a very refreshing summer drink."

The first "cock tails" were made by pouring whiskey over a sugar cube and adding some bitters. Although the origin of the term cocktail is in dispute, all sources suggest that it is American, possibly originating from a bar in Virginia whose owner served flavored drinks to Washington's soldiers and kept a jar of rooster tail feathers behind the bar. Perhaps these flavored wines allowed Victorian women, who would never drink spirits, to partake of a cocktail as well.

1 12-ounce package frozen blackberries
3 cups sugar
2 3-inch cinnamon sticks
1 1/2 teaspoons ground nutmeg

Yield: 1 1/2 pints concentrate
Mix blackberries and sugar in a heavy 2-quart saucepan. Bring to a boil over medium heat, stirring until the sugar is dissolved. Remove from heat and let stand until cool. Strain through a colander lined with cheesecloth or a jelly bag. Return to saucepan. Add spices and bring to a boil. Boil over medium heat until reduced by half. Strain and put in clean jars and keep in the refrigerator. To serve: Mix 1 or 2 Tablespoons to a glass of water or soda and serve over ice.

38 Calories per Tablespoon: Fat .2 g, Saturated fat 0 g, Cholesterol 0 mg, Sodium 7 mg.

Red Raspberry Shrub

2 12-ounce packages frozen raspberries
1 cup distilled vinegar
2 cups sugar (or more)

Yield: 1 1/2 pints concentrate

Put thawed raspberries in glass jar with vinegar. Let the jar stand in a cool place 2 or 3 days, giving it an occasional shake. Mash berries and strain through cheesecloth or jelly bag. Measure the juice and pour into a heavy saucepan. Stir in twice as much sugar as there is juice. Bring to a boil slowly. Reduce heat and simmer, stirring occasionally, for 20 minutes. Pour into hot sterilized jars and seal. To serve: Mix 1 or 2 Tablespoons to a glass of water or soda and serve over ice.

23 Calories per Tablespoon: Fat .14 g, Saturated fat 0 g, Cholesterol 0 mg, Sodium 10 mg.

There are other harvest drinks mentioned in Victorian American cookbooks. One is simply a very thin, sweetened oatmeal gruel. Packing more nutrition than refreshment, that beverage served as a meal in a glass so that workers could keep up their energy during hectic times in the fields.

Grandmother's Harvest Drink

I drink Grandmother's Harvest Drink as a pick-me-up after mowing our yard in the summer. I should caution you, it is very strong and acidic. I would not suggest it to anyone with a sensitive stomach.

2 Tablespoons sugar
1 1/2 teaspoons ground ginger
1/2 cup white vinegar
8 cups water

Yield: 16 1/2-cup servings
Mix the sugar and the ginger. Slowly add the vinegar, stirring until the ginger and sugar are dissolved. Combine with water and refrigerate. To serve: The ginger may settle out, so shake or stir the drink before pouring over ice.

8 Calories: Fat 0 g, Saturated fat 0 g, Cholesterol 0 mg, Sodium 0 mg.

Ham Puffs

Yes, a low-fat puff pastry. Unlike traditional cream puff recipes, the original recipe called for just three whole eggs and no butter. To reduce the fat content even more, I took out the egg yolks as well. Ham Puffs are best served hot, and are quite tasty stuffed with the cheese mixture below. I make these small to assure the inside cooks through.

1 cup water
1 cup flour
4 egg whites
1/4 cup ham, minced
dash cayenne pepper or to taste

Yield: 48 small puffs

Preheat oven to 400°F. In a heavy 2-quart pot, bring the water to a boil. Add the flour all at once and stir until combined. Add the egg whites, one by one. Stir well after each addition until the mixture is smooth. Stir in the ham and pepper. Drop the mixture by 1/2 teaspoonfuls onto cookie sheets. Bake for 10 minutes and then lower the oven temperature to 350°F. Bake until firm to the touch, about another 20 minutes or so. Remove from the oven and carefully cut a small slit in the top of each puff to allow steam to escape. Eat plain or stuffed with a savory filling such as the Cheese Mixture for Sandwiches (see below).

18 Calories each: Fat .38 g, Saturated fat .11 g, Cholesterol 13 mg, Sodium 11 mg.

Cheese Mixture for Sandwiches

4 ounces nonfat cream cheese
4 teaspoons dry mustard
2 teaspoons Hungarian paprika
2 cups low-fat cheddar cheese
1/4 cup lemon juice

This is a fairly hot mixture; cut back on the mustard and paprika if you don't like spicy foods. The original recipe used melted butter as a binder, but nonfat cream cheese works just as well.

Yield: 2 1/2 cups
Soften the cream cheese. Combine all ingredients in a food processor and process until smooth. (You can also mix the ingredients with an electric mixer or by hand.) Chill and spread on hearty bread or crackers.

36 calories per Tablespoon: Fat 2.4 g, Saturated fat 1 g, Cholesterol 6.5 mg, Sodium 45 mg.

Ginger Sandwiches

Mrs. F.'s Gingerbread (p. 72), cut in 1-inch squares
1 8-ounce package nonfat cream cheese
1/4 cup candied ginger

Yield: 84 appetizer sandwiches
Carefully split the gingerbread squares in half. Spread bottom half with softened nonfat cream cheese and thin slices of candied ginger. Replace the top slice and garnish with a swirl of cream cheese and a slice of candied ginger. For variation, try mixing a little minced ham with the cream cheese filling.

67 Calories: Fat .25 g, Saturated fat .15 g, Cholesterol 13.9 mg, Sodium 36.8 mg.

Deviled Mushroom Spread

1 1/2 cups fresh mushrooms, chopped
1 teaspoon cayenne pepper or to taste
3 Tablespoons lemon juice
2 teaspoons prepared French-style mustard or to taste
2 hard-boiled egg yolks
2 uncooked egg whites
1 cup bread crumbs
1 Tablespoon butter, melted
1/4 cup bread crumbs, additional
1 Tablespoon melted butter, additional

Yield: 48 2-Tablespoon servings
Preheat oven to 325°F. In a food processor, combine all the ingredients except the last 1/4 cup bread crumbs and a Tablespoon of melted butter. Pulse until just blended. Put the mixture in an ovenproof serving dish. Combine the remaining crumbs and melted butter and sprinkle over the top. Bake for 20 to 25 minutes, or until the mixture is firm like a pâté. Serve with crackers or hearty bread.

19 Calories per serving: Fat .83 g, Saturated fat .39 g, Cholesterol 9.9 mg, Sodium 29 mg.

Mrs. Kellogg's Fruit Sandwiches

2 Tablespoons nonfat cream cheese
2 Tablespoons stewed prunes, chopped or 1/2 ripe
    banana, sliced
2 slices graham or whole wheat bread

Yield: 1 sandwich
Combine the cream cheese and prunes, or banana slices, and spread between thin slices of bread.

272 Calories: Fat 8 g, Saturated fat 5 g, Cholesterol 23 mg,
Sodium 411 mg.

At the Kellogg Sanitarium in Battle Creek, Michigan, Mrs. E.E. Kellogg, wife of the founder, directed the kitchens in making "scientific" healthful foods. These recipes relied on whole grains and vegetables instead of white flour and meats.

Cut these sandwiches into quarters or shapes and serve as an appetizer.

Mrs. Kellogg's Egg Sandwiches

2 Tablespoons nonfat cream cheese
3 hard-boiled egg yolks, chopped
2 Tablespoons celery, minced
2 slices graham or whole wheat bread

Yield: 1 sandwich
Combine the cream cheese, egg yolks, and celery. Spread between thin slices of bread.

390 Calories: Fat 23 g, Saturated fat 9 g, Cholesterol 638 mg,
Sodium 444 mg.

Sauces and Pickles

Remember, the word relish means to enjoy, and the importance of a relish — both as a side dish and as an ingredient — should not be underestimated. For, as Mrs. E.F. Haskell suggests, fancy desserts take just as much effort to prepare and are consumed in one sitting. With relishes, the cook's efforts are rewarded with a product that lasts for weeks and adds important flavor counterpoints to both everyday meals and party menus. Mrs. E.F. Haskell and other Victorian cookbook authors published scores of condiment recipes including cucumber, lemon, and oyster ketchups. These sauces, along with fresh celery in celery jars, pickled vegetables, fruit chutneys, and flavored vinegars, were important side dishes at every Victorian dinner.

The earliest Victorian ketchups were thin vegetable extracts seasoned with herbs and spices. As the century continued, ketchup recipes expanded to include pickled, simmered fruit or vegetable purees more like today's heavier tomato ketchup. But even though the consistency may be similar, the flavor is not. The Victorian Tomato Ketchup tastefully illustrates the difference. This rich mahogany sauce is simple to make and has become a staple in my kitchen.

While the Strawberry Pickles may seem a bit fussy to make at first, they are well worth the effort. In this chapter I have also included recipes for spice and herb vinegars and two flavored gravies which make ideal dipping sauces for hot hors d'oeuvres. You will find sweet sauces for use with cakes and ice cream in the last two chapters.

Tomato Ketchup

2 28-ounce cans tomato puree
1 1/2 cups distilled vinegar
1/2 cup water
2 1/4 teaspoons ground cloves
4 teaspoons ground allspice
4 teaspoons ground cayenne pepper

Yield: 2 1/2 pints

Mix all ingredients in a heavy stockpot. Bring to a boil and reduce heat. Cook 2 to 3 hours, stirring occasionally until the mixture is reduced by half. You will need to stir more frequently at the end of the cooking time to keep the mixture from sticking to the bottom of the pot. Pour into clean, sterilized jars and seal. Keeps for a month in the refrigerator.

11 Calories per Tablespoon: Fat 0 g, Saturated fat 0 g, Cholesterol 0 mg, Sodium 4.2 mg

If you intend to keep these sauces for longer than the time specified, it is vital that you put them into sterilized jars and follow standard canning procedures, or keep them frozen.

If you are tired of flat-tasting modern ketchups, try this Victorian version. In addition to being a terrific topper for hamburgers and hot dogs, it can be substituted for ketchup in any sauce or stew recipe.

Delmonico's Sauce for Meats

2 Tablespoons butter
1 ounce ham, finely minced
1 onion, finely minced
1 carrot, finely minced
2 Tablespoons flour
2 cups water
1 teaspoon pepper
3/4 cup sherry

Forget the gigantic steaks and chops, this sauce alone would have put Delmonico's New York steak house on the map. The ingredients are deceptively simple, and the combination makes a wonderful low-fat alternative to regular gravy.

Yield: 3 cups

Melt the butter in a medium saucepan. Add the ham, carrot, and onion. Sauté until the onion is transparent. Add the flour and cook until lightly browned. Slowly add the water, stirring constantly, until sauce is smooth. Simmer for 1 hour, and then process in a blender or food processor until smooth. Add the pepper and sherry and mix well. Serve with meats.

13 Calories per Tablespoon: Fat .53 g, Saturated fat .30 g, Cholesterol 2 mg, Sodium 12 mg.

Cucumber Ketchup

3 large cucumbers, peeled, seeded, and grated
1 onion, peeled and minced
1 Tablespoon salt
2 1/2 teaspoons black pepper
1 1/2 cups white vinegar

Yield: 1 pint

Mix the cucumbers and onions with salt. Put the vegetables into a cheesecloth-lined colander and let stand 1 hour. Pour out drained juices and gently squeeze the vegetable mixture until dry. If you want to reduce the salt content, you may rinse off the vegetable mixture before you squeeze it dry. Mix the vegetables, vinegar, and pepper in a heavy stockpot. Cook gently until the mixture is hot and has turned somewhat yellow. Cool and then carefully process in a food processor or blender until smooth. Return to the stockpot and simmer until thick, stirring to prevent sticking as it reduces and thickens. Pour into clean, sterilized jars and seal. Keeps up to two months in the refrigerator.

11 Calories per Tablespoon: Fat 0 g, Saturated fat 0 g, Cholesterol 0 mg, Sodium 219 mg.

It is hard to imagine that the spiciness of this snappy condiment comes from vinegar and black pepper. Try spreading it on a ham on whole wheat sandwich cut into quarters for an easy appetizer.

Pineapple Marmalade

1 large pineapple
4 cups sugar

Yield: 2 pints

Peel, core, and process the pineapple in a food processor until it is a fine dice. Combine the pineapple and sugar in equal amounts in a heavy stockpot. Cook over medium heat, stirring occasionally, until thick. Bottle in sterilized jars. This keeps in the refrigerator for 2 months.

87 Calories per Tablespoon: Fat .13 g, Saturated fat .01 g, Cholesterol 0 mg, Sodium .43 mg.

Pineapples have been an American symbol of hospitality since colonial days. Grown in Cuba during the nineteenth century, they were probably as common then as they are now.

This spread is simple to make and is a delight on breakfast toast, with cream cheese as a tea sandwich, or for dessert over a plain cake.

Ever-Ready Ketchup

Because you drain off all of the vegetable and spice solids, these two ketchups are very thin. But don't let the consistency fool you, both ketchups have very strong flavors. A little goes a long way.

8 cups cider vinegar
12 anchovies
1 Tablespoon mace
2 Tablespoons salt
3 Tablespoons sugar
1 Tablespoon whole cloves
3 whole black peppercorns
4 cups mushrooms, minced

Yield: 3 pints
Combine all ingredients in a large stewpan. Bring to a boil, reduce heat, and simmer for 4 hours or until reduced by half. Strain through several layers of cheesecloth and bottle in clean, sterilized jars. Keeps for 2 months in the refrigerator.

19 Calories per Tablespoon: Fat .59 g, Saturated fat .13 g, Cholesterol 5 mg, Sodium 352 mg.

Lemon Ketchup

12 lemons
1/4 cup whole mustard seeds
1 Tablespoon turmeric
1 Tablespoon white pepper
1 teaspoon whole cloves
1 teaspoon ground mace
1/3 teaspoon cayenne pepper
2 Tablespoons sugar

2 Tablespoons horseradish (not cream-style)
1 shallot, minced
2 teaspoons salt, or less to taste

Yield: 2 cups
Grate the yellow part of the rind from the lemons
and squeeze out all of the juice. Combine the grated
rind and juice with the other ingredients in a medium saucepan. Simmer gently for 20 minutes to
extract the flavors. Strain the ketchup through several layers of cheesecloth into sterilized bottles. Keeps
for up to 2 months in the refrigerator.

21 Calories per Tablespoon: Fat .05 g, Saturated fat .03 g,
Cholesterol 0 mg, Sodium 146 mg.

*Every Victorian kitchen
had its own supply of "store
sauces." These vinegars are
easy to make.
Substitute them for plain
vinegar in salad dressings
and coleslaw recipes. A
tablespoon or two added to
soup, chili, or stew can make
a remarkable difference.*

Clove Vinegar

*Bottled in sterilized jars,
these vinegars will keep for
several months in a cool,
dry place.*

2 ounces whole cloves
4 cups vinegar

Yield: 4 Cups
Bruise the cloves gently with a mortar and pestle or
a hammer and a strong plastic bag. Put cloves in a
clean jar and add the vinegar. Let stand 6 weeks.
Repeatedly filter the vinegar through several layers
of cheesecloth or a lint-free cloth until it is free of
particles. Bottle in sterilized jars.

7 Calories per Tablespoon: Fat .17 g, Saturated fat .03 g,
Cholesterol 0 mg, Sodium 2.2 mg.

Basil Vinegar

4 cups fresh basil leaves
8 cups vinegar

Yield: 8 Cups

Put vinegar and the basil leaves in a glass jar. Set the jar in the sun for 2 weeks. Drain off the vinegar, pressing the basil leaves thoroughly. If you want a stronger taste, add more fresh basil leaves and repeat the process until the vinegar reaches the desired flavor. Bottle in sterilized jars with a couple of fresh basil leaves for decoration.

4 Calories per Tablespoon: Fat 0 g, Saturated fat 0 g, Cholesterol 0 mg, Sodium .2 mg.

Piquant Sauce

2 Tablespoons capers
2 Tablespoons onions, minced
1 cup vinegar
2 Tablespoons butter
2 Tablespoons flour
2 cups beef stock

Yield: 3 cups

In a small saucepan, combine the capers, onion, and vinegar. Simmer for 30 minutes or until the vinegar is reduced to 1/4 cup. Add the butter and allow it to melt. Stir in the flour and cook over low heat until it becomes frothy. Then, gradually add the beef stock.

Continue cooking, stirring until thickened. Serve with beef or pork chops.

7 Calories per : Fat .5 g, Saturated fat .31 g,1.3 mg, Sodium 42g.

Strawberry Pickles

1 teaspoon ground cinnamon
1 teaspoon ground cloves
2 quarts strawberries
3/4 cup cider vinegar
2 cups sugar

Yield: 2 pints

Combine the cinnamon and cloves. Wash berries and blot them dry. Remove the stems, and cut large berries in half. Discard any bruised or soft berries. Cover the bottom of a large, heatproof glass bowl, or other nonreactive container, with a layer of strawberries and sprinkle with some of the cinnamon and clove mixture. Continue making layers until you have used up all the berries and spices. Combine the vinegar and sugar. Bring to a boil and cook for 10 minutes. Gradually pour the syrup over the berries, cover the container, and let stand in a cool place for 24 hours. Pour off the syrup, bring to a boil, and pour back over the berries. Let the berries stand as before for another 24 hours. The next day, simmer the berries in the syrup gently for 25 minutes. Bottle in sterilized jars and keep in refrigerator for up to 2 months.

These are wonderfully versatile pickles, and are well worth the three days it takes to make them. They are a tasty side dish and make a nice garnish for ham, cheese, or open-faced chicken sandwiches. These are a little runny just after you make them, but they thicken up after a week or so. Note: After you finish the pickles, save the juice and mix with water to make a Strawberry Shrub. Follow the Red Raspberry Shrub recipe (p. 3).

32 Calories per Tablespoon: Fat .23 g, Saturated fat .07 g, Cholesterol 0 mg, Sodium 1.1 mg.

Soups

"Good soup should appear on the dinner table every day of the year and would be found to be the healthiest diet for young and old."

Eliza Parker
Good Housekeeping, March 1885

As the authors of many Victorian housekeeping handbooks suggested, French families could live for a week on food the typical Victorian American family discarded. These handbooks described how vegetables, scraps of meat, even the bones of Porterhouse steak, could be put to good use preparing stews, hashes, and — most importantly — soups.

Three types of soups were popular during the Victorian era: hearty soups and chowders filled with diced meats and vegetables; broth soups served as a first or second course; and soups "after the French manner," in which the vegetables were simmered in stock until tender, then pureed. In almost all of the soup recipes I have reviewed and tested, the cook is carefully instructed to begin making the soup stock with meat and bones in cold water and not to allow the pot to come to a boil for at least one hour. This assures the meat juices and nutrients are fully extracted. The cook was also urged to remove and discard every bit of fat from the stock before continuing with the recipe.

Victorians were not of one mind regarding the place soups should have in the diet. Many authors suggested that soup should be eaten by invalids. Others, including Catherine Beecher, suggested that soup was not suitable for persons "with weak stomachs." However, Sarah Hale, editor of *Godey's Ladies Book* unequivocally stated that, "Every dinner must begin with soup." The soups in this chapter include all three kinds of Victorian soups. Of particular interest are Bob the Sea-Cook's Bean Soup and the Pocket Soup prepared by Amelia Murray, an Englishwoman traveling in upstate New York in 1885.

Clam Chowder

5 slices bacon, chopped
3 cups clams
3/4 teaspoon cayenne pepper or to taste
3 Tablespoons butter, melted
1 1/2 cups onions, sliced
1 1/2 cups oyster crackers, finely crushed
1 1/2 cups milk
8 cups water (approximately)
1 cup white wine
1/2 cup Tomato Ketchup (p. 10)

Yield: 12 1-cup servings
Fry the bacon crisp and drain off the fat. Put bacon bits in the bottom of a large pot. Add 1 cup clams, and sprinkle with 1/4 teaspoon cayenne pepper and 1 Tablespoon melted butter. Put 1/2 cup sliced onions on top of the clams. Cover with 1/2 cup of the crushed oyster crackers and moisten with 1/2 cup milk. Repeat these layers 2 more times. Add water until the layers are just covered. Put a lid on the pot and stew very slowly over low heat for 1 hour. Add the wine and ketchup, and stir to mix well.

171 Calories: Fat 4.8 g, Saturated fat 1.3 g, Cholesterol 33.7 mg, Sodium 359 mg.

Many Victorian cookbooks urged their readers to remove every bit of fat from soup stock. Rather than adding fat back by using a flour and butter roux, the Victorian cook frequently used bread crumbs or crushed crackers to thicken soups. The key to the success of this thickening method is crushing the crackers very finely.

This chowder is a nice compromise between creamy New England chowder and the tomato-based Manhattan version. It is very light and satisfying.

18

Carrot Soup

1 pound beef soup bones
4 cups carrots, finely chopped
1 bunch celery
3 quarts cold water
1 cup uncooked rice

Mrs. E.E. Kellogg of Battle Creek, Michigan, wrote, "The use of large quantities of animal food . . . has a tendency to develop the animal propensities . . . especially in the young whose characters are unformed." This vegetable soup uses only a minimal amount of meat to add flavor to the carrots and rice.

Yield: 12 1-cup servings
Put the soup bones, carrots, and celery in the water. Bring to a boil and simmer for 2 hours, skimming if necessary. Remove the beef bones and cut off any meat. Return the meat to the stock. Add the rice and simmer until the rice is tender, about 20 to 25 minutes. Season with pepper or hot sauce, if desired.

139 Calories: Fat 3.4 g, Saturated fat 1.3 g, Cholesterol 1.3 mg, Sodium 107 mg.

Apple Soup

Victorians did not limit their soup ingredients to vegetables and meat. There were several kinds of fruit soups that were served hot in the winter and cold in the summer. If an apple a day keeps the doctor away and chicken soup is good for colds, imagine what good can come from this very simple soup!

3 large apples (about 1 pound)
3 whole cloves
1 Tablespoon dried onion
6 cups chicken stock
1/4 teaspoon celery seeds
1/4 cup carrots, grated
1/2 teaspoon pepper
1/2 teaspoon ground ginger
1/4 teaspoon ground cloves

Yield: 6 1-cup servings

Peel and quarter the apples and remove the cores. Stick the cloves in one of the pieces of apple. Put the apples, dried onion, and chicken stock in a large, heavy pot. Stew gently until tender, about 45 minutes. Remove the whole cloves from the apple slice and discard the cloves. Carefully puree the apples. Return apples to the stock and add the remaining ingredients. Simmer for 10 minutes and serve.

109 Calories: Fat 1.6 g, Saturated fat .39 g, Cholesterol 0 mg, Sodium 146 mg.

Mrs. Murray's Pocket Soup

4 cups water
4 cubes beef bouillon
1 medium sweet onion, 1/4-inch dice
2 medium potatoes, 1/4-inch dice
3 Tablespoons sweet wine
1 Tablespoon arrowroot
4 biscuits, split

Yield: 4 1-cup servings

Bring water to a boil and add the bouillon cubes, onions, and potatoes. Lower heat and simmer for 20 to 30 minutes, or until the vegetables are tender. Mix the arrowroot and the wine. Pour into the hot soup and stir until thickened. Put two biscuit halves in a bowl and pour soup over them.

425 Calories: Fat 13.5 g, Saturated fat 8.8 g, Cholesterol 5.3 mg, Sodium 810 mg.

During the 1800s, travelers in the United States frequently carried "portable soup" as the only safe and tasty food they could obtain as they journeyed away from major coastal cities. Also called "pocket soup," this highly evaporated beef bouillon was dried in sheets and broken off as needed. In 1885 an Englishwoman named Amelia Murray wrote about the soup in her travel journal from her camp on the shores of Lake Saranac, New York: "Our tent was pitched behind a gigantic fallen tree . . . it served as a convenient table for our cooking operation. I made a can of excellent portable soup, a provision we had tried before with success."

20

Mock Turtle Bean Soup

Recipes for Turtle Soup are plentiful in Victorian cookbooks and involve getting a large turtle and dealing with it appropriately. Inland residents could convert a calf's head into mock turtle soup by following a page and a half of directions. Needless to say, I was delighted to find this recipe. Perhaps this is why black beans are sometimes called turtle beans. This soup is just as good, if not better, the second day.

1 pound black beans
3 quarts cold water
1 onion, sliced
1/4 teaspoon pepper
1 dash cayenne pepper
1/4 teaspoon dry mustard
1/2 teaspoon ground cloves
1/2 teaspoon ground allspice
1/4 teaspoon ground cinnamon
1 Tablespoon parsley
1/2 teaspoon ground marjoram
1 Tablespoon flour
2 Tablespoons butter
1 cup sherry or white wine
Forcemeat Balls (p. 23)
2 hard-boiled eggs, separated
1 lemon, sliced

Yield: 12 1-cup servings
Wash the beans, removing any foreign material. Put the beans in a large pot, cover with cold water, and soak overnight. In the morning, drain off the water and rinse. Put the beans in a large pot with the 3 quarts cold water. Add the onion and simmer 4 or 5 hours, or until the beans are very soft. Add more cold water as needed to keep the beans covered. Rub the beans and cooking liquid through a strainer and put the soup on to boil again, adding the spices and herbs. In a small mixing bowl, blend the flour with the softened butter. As the soup comes to a boil, add the flour mixture bit by bit to thicken the soup. Stir in the wine and Forcemeat Balls. Grate the egg whites and yolks separately. Garnish the soup with the grated egg and lemon slices.

94 Calories: Fat 3 g, Saturated fat 1.5 g, Cholesterol 41 mg, Sodium 121 mg.

Mulligatawny Soup

1 whole chicken
1 pound beef soup bones
4 quarts cold water
2 onions, sliced
2 tart apples, peeled and chopped
1 teaspoon sugar
1 Tablespoon curry powder
1/2 teaspoon ground cloves
1 1/2 teaspoons pepper
1 lemon, juiced
1 cup uncooked rice

Yield: 16 1-cup servings

Cut the chicken into quarters. Put the chicken and beef bones into a large soup kettle and cover with cold water. Add the onions and apples. Combine the sugar, curry powder, cloves, and pepper and make into a paste with the juice from the lemon. Stir paste into the soup. Simmer for 2 hours, or until the chicken is tender. Remove the chicken and beef bones from the soup. Skim any visible fat from the soup stock. Cut meat into bite-size pieces, and return to the pot. Add rice to the soup pot and simmer for 25 minutes, or until the rice is soft.

250 Calories: Fat 12.2 g, Saturated fat 3.7 g, Cholesterol 100 mg, Sodium 82 mg.

The name of this stew-like soup means "pepper pot" in the Tamil dialect of Hindi. Soldiers and their families returning from postings in India popularized the flavors of the tropics in England. As English cookbooks were sold in this country, these foreign cuisines made their way into the American mainstream.

Forcemeat Balls

1 cup leftover cooked beef or other meat,
  finely chopped
1/4 teaspoon thyme
1/4 teaspoon pepper
1 teaspoon lemon juice
1 teaspoon dried parsley
1 egg
dash onion powder
1 Tablespoon flour
1 Tablespoon butter

Yield: 36 meatballs

Victorians enhanced and garnished many kinds of soups with Forcemeat Balls. They also make a nice appetizer when served with a sauce such as the Piquant Sauce (p. 15).

Combine ingredients except the flour and butter. Form the mixture into balls about the size of a marble (about a teaspoon of meat per meatball). Coat meatballs with flour. Melt the butter in a small frying pan. Gently fry the meatballs in the butter until they are browned. Add to soup, such as the Mulligatawny Soup (p. 22).

37 Calories each: Fat 1.8 g, Saturated fat .9 g, Cholesterol 25 mg, Sodium 183 mg.

Bob the Sea-Cook's Bean Soup

3 cups dried navy beans
3 pounds beef soup bones
4 quarts water
1 onion, sautéed in butter
6 whole cloves
12 small cayenne peppers
1 Tablespoon fresh parsley
3 hard-boiled eggs, diced
2 cups toasted French bread cubes

Yield: 12 1-cup servings

Wash the beans and sort to remove any foreign material. Soak overnight in water to cover. Drain. Add the beef bones and water, bring to a boil, and simmer for 30 minutes. Add the remaining ingredients – except the eggs and bread cubes – and continue to simmer for 2 hours, or until the beans are tender. Add water as necessary to keep beans covered. Remove the bone and meat. Strain the soup through a sieve, mashing the beans. Cut up the meat and return to the soup. Garnish with hard-boiled eggs and bread cubes.

320 Calories: Fat 10 g, Saturated fat 3.8 g, Cholesterol 90 mg, Sodium 92 mg.

Bean soup was a standby aboard ships; it was inexpensive to make, filling, and a good way to use available ingredients. According to Bob the Sea-Cook, who is quoted in Dr. Chase's Receipt Book, *"Bean soup is a mighty good thing, according to the way you make it. If you know how to turn it out, sailors will take three platefuls. If you happen to be cruising south," advised Bob, "just you use, instead of the New England bean, the Georgia or South Carolina cow-pea."*

The number of cayenne peppers called for in Bob's recipe may have been appropriate for warming up cold sailors on Boston whaling vessels, but it may be excessive for your taste. Use your own judgement on that score.

French Vegetable Soup

4 large baking potatoes, peeled and chopped
1 large parsnip, peeled and chopped
2 large onions, peeled and chopped
1 large carrot, peeled and chopped
6 quarts low-salt beef stock
1 teaspoon black pepper
1 teaspoon salt
3 Tablespoons Dijon mustard
1/2 cup Tomato Ketchup (p. 10)

Yield: 16 1-cup servings
Combine the vegetables with the stock in a large
kettle. Simmer until vegetables are tender, about
30 minutes. Remove the vegetables from the stock
and carefully process in batches in a food processor or blender until smooth. Return vegetables to
the stock and add the spices, mustard, and ketchup.
Heat through, being careful not to scorch the soup.

144 Calories: Fat 1.1 g, Saturated fat 0 g, Cholesterol 0 mg,
Sodium 441 mg.

Main Dishes and Vegetables

"The same 'plain cookery' is the pivot on which the family health and comfort rest and turn. . .
'Fancy' cookery is to the real thing what embroidery is to the art of the seamstress."

Marion Harland
Cookery for Beginners, 1884

Many Victorian era cookbooks published recipes drawn from the menus of high-society restaurants or estate dining rooms. Studying these books, it is easy to get the mistaken impression that every Victorian meal featured several courses, each with its specially selected wine, heavy sauces, and rich desserts. While these recipes are interesting to read, and even cook, they bear little resemblance to what was served to most Victorians.

Mrs. E.E. Kellogg of the Battle Creek, Michigan, health sanitarium and cereal company fame had strong opinions about the health problems caused by eating such rich foods. She advocated moderation and simple cooking in her 1898 cookbook, *Science in the Kitchen*. "Meat pies, scallops, sauces, fricassees, pâtés, and other fancy dishes composed of a mixture of animal foods, rich pastry, fats, strong condiments, etc., are by no means to be recommended as hygienic, and will receive no notice in these pages."

Other Victorian authors did publish recipes for the roasts, stews, and braised meat dishes that formed the foundation of American Victorian cooking. Vegetarians, or those simply seeking a balanced diet in the interest of avoiding dyspepsia, took advantage of an abundance of seasonal fresh vegetables throughout the Victorian era. Physicians recommended asparagus as particularly healthful. Peas, parsnips, turnips, carrots, beans, cabbage, cauliflower, squash, and dozens of other vegetables were grown in backyard gardens or purchased fresh from green grocers in the city.

Vegetables were most often simply boiled until tender. Tomatoes and cold lettuce salads became increasingly popular as the era drew to a close. By the turn of the century, the widespread availability of canned vegetables, fruits, meats, and seafood liberated cooks from the restrictions of seasonal availability.

26

In choosing recipes for this section I have tried to include those which reflect the variety of influences on Victorian American entrees and vegetables. The Pork, Parsnip, and Potato Hash is a simple stovetop or campfire dish while the Crab Olio is a more elaborate preparation, requiring less readily available ingredients. The Pilau and Chicken Curry are two dishes which boast exotic foreign influences. Cucumbers in Poulette Sauce, Creamed Carrots, and Tip-Top Potatoes round out the section with some examples of the different ways Victorian cooks dressed vegetables.

Company Dinner Including Children and Grown Folks

Sago Soup

Spring Chicken — Scalloped

Filet of Roast Beef

Sweet Breads

Stewed Mushrooms

Fried Potatoes

Lima Beans

Cauliflower

Corn Fritters

Tomato Salad

Blanc Mange with Cherries and Peaches

Currant Ice

Dessert Cakes

Cheese

Coffee

Good Housekeeping, September 5, 1885.

Ragout of Beef

2 onions, sliced
1 pound low-salt canned stewed tomatoes
3 pounds beef rump roast, trimmed of all visible fat
6 whole cloves
1 3-inch cinnamon stick
1/2 teaspoon whole black peppercorns
1/2 cup vinegar
1 cup water

Yield: 12 servings
This can be cooked in a crock pot or in the oven. If using your oven, preheat to 300°F. Place the sliced onions in the bottom of a slow cooker, or an oven-proof dish with a lid. Pour the tomatoes over the onions, and place the beef on top. Tie the spices in a clean piece of muslin or several layers of cheesecloth. Put the spices in the pot and add the vinegar and water. Cover the pot and cook on medium or low setting for 5 to 8 hours, or bake in oven for 4 to 5 hours, or until tender.

163 Calories: Fat 4 g, Saturated fat 1.4 g, Cholesterol 66 mg, Sodium 73 mg.

Tomatoes have become much less acidic over the past 50 years. To recapture the flavor and tenderizing ability of Victorian tomatoes, I have added a tablespoon more vinegar to the original recipe.

Beef à la Mode

The broth left over from make making this dish can be served as soup, or simply poured over the meat as a sauce. The secret to success-fully preparing this dish is cutting wide, shallow slits into the uncooked beef so that it can be properly stuffed.

4 slices bacon
2 onions, minced
1/4 teaspoon ground cloves
1/4 teaspoon ground allspice
1/2 teaspoon ground pepper
1/2 teaspoon ground savory
1/2 teaspoon ground thyme
1/2 teaspoon ground tarragon
3 pounds flank steak
2 carrots, sliced
1 turnip, diced
1 bunch celery, sliced
3 cups water
3/4 cup port wine

Yield: 8 servings

Dice the bacon slices and fry in a frying pan over low heat. When the pan is covered with bacon drippings, add the onion and continue cooking over medium heat until the bacon bits are crisp and the onion is transparent. Remove from heat and drain off fat. Blot with paper towels to eliminate as much fat as possible. Set aside to cool. Combine the spices and set aside. With a sharp knife, cut the surface of the flank steak, making five or six cuts lengthwise across the piece of meat. Hold the knife at an angle so that the cut is more parallel than perpendicular to the surface of the meat. Do not cut completely through the piece of meat. Rub the spices into the slits. Stuff the slits with onion and bacon. Roll the meat into a cylinder from the long edge, parallel to the cuts. Tie securely with kitchen string. Put the meat roll into a stewpot or slow cooker.

Add the vegetables, water, and wine. Simmer very slowly for 5 hours, or until the meat is tender. When tender, transfer the meat and vegetables from the pot to a heated plate. Allow to stand for 10 minutes. Cut the meat across the grain in slices so that the pinwheel of spices, onions, and bacon shows. Remove all the fat from the broth, and serve broth as a soup or as a sauce over the vegetables and meat.

362 Calories: Fat 15.2 g, Saturated fat 4.2 g, Cholesterol 89 mg, Sodium 291 mg.

Pork, Parsnip, and Potato Hash

2 cups parsnips, 1/2-inch dice
1 cup potato, 1/2-inch dice
3/4 cup cooked pork, 1/4-inch dice
2 Tablespoons butter
1 Tablespoon oil

Parsnips look like white carrots. They were a staple vegetable during the Victorian period, especially in the South. Parsnips harvested after the frost are thought to be sweeter. Look for parsnips which are firm and clean, and do not overcook them.

Yield: 3 servings
Boil the parsnips and potato for 15 minutes or until the pieces are crisp-tender. Drain well. Combine the pork with the vegetables. Heat the butter and oil in a heavy frying pan. When hot, but not smoking, add the meat and vegetable hash. Cover and cook over low heat until crust forms on the bottom of the hash. Then broil hash briefly to brown the top. Serve with applesauce or leftover gravy.

288 Calories: Fat 15 g, Saturated fat 6 g, Cholesterol 43 mg, Sodium 106 mg.

Scalloped Chicken

2 pounds new potatoes
2 pounds skinless, boneless chicken breasts or other
        chicken parts
2 cups water (approximately)
1 egg, lightly beaten
2 Tablespoons cornstarch
1 cup milk
2 Tablespoons butter
1/2 cup cracker crumbs, finely crushed
2 Tablespoons butter, additional

Yield: 8 servings

Preheat oven to 350°F. Boil the unpeeled and well-scrubbed potatoes until tender. Stew the chicken parts for 20 minutes in just enough water to cover them. Remove the chicken from the broth. In a small mixing bowl, combine the egg and cornstarch with the milk. Slowly pour the milk mixture into the broth. Cook over low heat until the broth is thickened. Layer half the potatoes, sliced in 1/4-inch thick slices and half the chicken, cut into bite-size pieces. Cover this layer with half of the thickened broth and repeat the layers. Combine 2 Tablespoons butter with cracker crumbs. Crumble over top of casserole, and drizzle the remaining butter over the top. Bake in an uncovered dish for 20 to 30 minutes.

373 Calories: Fat 11.4 g, Saturated fat 3.3 g, Cholesterol 123 mg, Sodium 216 mg.

Corn and Chicken

1 broiler-fryer chicken, cut in serving pieces
2 Tablespoons flour
1/2 teaspoon thyme
1/2 teaspoon black pepper
1 cup milk
1 14-ounce can cream-style corn

Yield: 6 servings

Preheat oven to 350°F. Remove the skin from the chicken pieces. Combine the flour, thyme, and pepper. Dust the chicken lightly with flour and spice mixture. Put the chicken, meaty side down, in a casserole dish large enough to hold it in a single layer. Pour the milk over the chicken. Cover and bake, until the chicken is almost done, about 45 minutes. Turn the chicken pieces over and pour the corn around them. Return to oven until the corn is cooked through and the sauce has begun to thicken slightly.

363 Calories: Fat 18 g, Saturated fat 5.3 g, Cholesterol 123 mg, Sodium 111 mg.

Corn was one of the first vegetables to be sold in tin cans in the United States. According to Earl Chapin May's **The Canning Clan,** *the first shipment of Winslow's Maine Corn in "canisters" was sold to Samuel S. Pierce of Boston in 1848 for $4.00. By the 1880s canned American fruits, vegetables, meats, and seafood were being sold affordably and profitably across the country and around the world.*

32

Crab Olio

6 tomatoes (about 1 pound), peeled, seeded,
    and diced (If you cannot find good and
    flavorful fresh tomatoes, use canned
    stewed tomatoes.)
1 medium eggplant, peeled and diced
2 Tablespoons vinegar
1 cup crab meat
1/2 cup bread crumbs
1/2 teaspoon black pepper
3 eggs
2 Tablespoons butter
1/2 cup bread crumbs, additional

Not to be confused with "oleo" — the substitute for butter — the name of this late Victorian dish probably comes from the Spanish olla podrida. An olla is a large earthen pot and podrida means rotten, referring to the pungent spicy stews popular in Spain during the 1700s. In later years, olla came to mean a dish of varied ingredients. It is hard to imagine a mixture as unexpected as eggplant, crab, and tomato.

Crab Olio is good served hot or slightly above room temperature. It serves eight as an appetizer or four as a main course.

Yield: 4 servings

Preheat oven to 350°F. Drain excess liquid from tomatoes. Microwave the eggplant and vinegar in a covered container at medium power for 5 minutes, or until tender. While the eggplant is cooking, pick through the crab meat, removing any bits of shell or cartilage. Combine tomatoes with crab, bread crumbs, pepper, and eggplant. Lightly beat eggs and stir into this mixture. Put the mixture into decorative crab shells or individual ramekins. Melt the butter and combine it with the remaining half cup crumbs. Put the crumb topping over the crab mixture and bake until warmed through and the top is brown, about 15 minutes.

311 Calories: Fat 11.9 g, Saturated fat 5.1 g, Cholesterol 195 mg, Sodium 686 mg.

Carrots in Cream Sauce

4 cups carrots, scraped and cut in 1/2-inch slices
1 1/2 cups water (approximately)
1 teaspoon sugar
2 Tablespoons butter
1 Tablespoon flour
1 1/2 cups milk
1 1/2 teaspoons pepper

Yield: 8 servings

Cook carrot slices in enough water to cover them until just tender. Drain off water, reserving 1/2 cup. Sprinkle carrots with sugar, set aside, and keep warm. In a saucepan, melt the butter and stir in the flour, cooking until it is bubbly. Gradually add the milk and reserved carrot water. Cook until the sauce is thickened, about 5 minutes. Add the pepper. Pour sauce over carrots, stir gently, and serve.

87 Calories: Fat 4.5 g, Saturated fat 2.8 g, Cholesterol 13.9 mg, Sodium 71 mg.

Most vegetables were prepared simply throughout the Victorian era. They were boiled and served hot or cold, dressed with a vinaigrette dressing. The only significant difference I've found between the way Victorians prepared vegetables and the way we do today is in the amount of time recommended for cooking vegetables. The Victorian cook was advised to prepare carrots by discarding the center of the root and cooking the remainder for 1 to 2 hours. When I read the description of Victorian era carrots as being "2 feet in length and 2 inches wide," these lengthy cooking times began to make sense.

34

Potato Pie

1 cup baking potato, grated
4 cups milk
3 eggs
1/4 cup sugar
1 teaspoon ground nutmeg

Yield: 16 servings
Preheat oven to 350°F. Peel the potatoes and grate them directly into the milk. Lightly beat the eggs and sugar. Add to the potato mixture with the nutmeg. Pour into two lightly greased, 9-inch pie pans. Bake for 1 hour, or until firm.

75 Calories: Fat 3 g, Saturated fat 1.6 g, Cholesterol 46 mg, Sodium 43 mg.

Tip-Top Potatoes

1 pound new potatoes
2 lemons
2 Tablespoons butter
1 teaspoon low-sodium beef bouillon powder
1 teaspoon parsley, finely chopped
1/2 teaspoon pepper

Yield: 4 servings
Boil the potatoes in their skins until tender. While potatoes are boiling, grate the rinds of the lemons and set aside. Cut potatoes into quarters or bite-size pieces, depending upon their size. Place in a

microwavable serving dish and set aside. Melt the butter in a small saucepan and add the bouillon, parsley, pepper, and the grated rinds of the lemons. Squeeze the juice from both lemons over the potatoes. Stir the sauce until well blended and pour over the potatoes. Heat in the microwave until piping hot.

189 Calories: Fat 6 g, Saturated fat 3.7 g, Cholesterol 16 mg, Sodium 125 mg.

Tip-Top Potato Salad

2 cups new potatoes
2 lemons
2 Tablespoons oil
1 teaspoon beef bouillon powder
1 teaspoon parsley
2 Tablespoons vinegar
1/2 teaspoon pepper

The lemon really comes through strongly in these recipes. If you don't like lemon all that much, reduce the amount of lemon peel.

Yield: 4 servings
Boil the potatoes in their skins until tender. Grate the lemon rinds, and squeeze out the juice from both lemons. Combine the juice and grated rinds with the remaining ingredients. When the potatoes are cooked and slightly cooled, peel and cut them into 1-inch cubes. Pour the dressing over the warm potatoes, cover the dish, and allow to cool at room temperature. Stir occasionally so that the dressing is evenly absorbed by the potatoes.

148 Calories: Fat 7 g, Saturated fat .082 mg, Cholesterol 0 mg, Sodium 54 mg.

Chicken Curry

Popular acceptance of dishes such as the curry and pilau on these pages reflect a Victorian interest in foreign cooking. However, such foods were not wholeheartedly embraced by all. In her guide, American Woman's Home, *Catherine Beecher urged selectivity in serving foreign dishes on American tables. "Half of the recipes in our cookbooks are mere murder to such constitutions and stomachs as we grow here . . . (however) we may take some leaves from many foreign books."*

This is a very mild curry. Serve it with rice, fruit salad, Strawberry Pickles (p. 16), or a commercially prepared chutney.

6 skinless, boneless chicken breast
        halves or other chicken parts
1/2 teaspoon pepper
1/3 cup flour
2 Tablespoons butter
2 Tablespoons oil
1 large onion, thinly sliced
1 Tablespoon flour, additional
1 teaspoon sugar
1 Tablespoon curry powder
1 cup chicken stock
1 tart apple, peeled, cored, and chopped
1 cup milk

Yield: 6 servings

Season the chicken with pepper to taste and dust with flour. Put the butter and oil in a large frying pan and heat over medium heat until hot, but not smoking. Add the chicken carefully and brown on both sides. Remove from pan and set aside. Slowly cook the onion slices in the remaining oil until they are transparent. Add the flour, sugar, and curry powder. Cook, stirring constantly, until the flour is lightly browned. Slowly add the stock and stir until the flour and spices are combined and the sauce begins to thicken. Return the chicken to the pan along with any juices that have accumulated on the plate. Add the chopped apple. Cover and simmer over low heat until the chicken is done, about 30 minutes. Remove the chicken to a serving plate, and add the milk to the sauce. Boil sauce for one minute, stirring constantly. Pour over the chicken.

324 Calories: Fat 13.7 g, Saturated fat 4.6 g, Cholesterol 96 mg, Sodium 374 mg.

Pilau

2 cups uncooked rice
2 Tablespoons butter
1 broiler-fryer chicken, cut in pieces or 3 pounds
     boneless chicken parts
4 cups low-sodium chicken stock
1 teaspoon ground cardamom
1/2 teaspoon ground coriander
1/4 teaspoon ground cloves
1/4 teaspoon ground allspice
1/4 teaspoon ground mace
1/4 teaspoon ground cinnamon
1/2 teaspoon ground black pepper
6 ounces sliced extra lean ham, cut in bite-size pieces
2 hard-boiled eggs, sliced
1 2.8-ounce can french fried onions

Some sources suggest this dish came to the Carolinas with the China spice traders. Certainly it is related to a wide variety of Middle Eastern pilafs. In the orginal version, the cook was directed to fry the onions herself. The canned french fried onions are just as good and save the cook a lot of time and trouble.

Yield: 8 servings

Put the rice in a frying pan with the butter and cook over low heat, stirring frequently, until the rice is lightly browned. Place the chicken parts in the chicken stock with the spices and simmer over low heat until done, about 30 minutes. Remove the chicken and skim all the visible fat from the stock. Remove the bones and the skin from the chicken and cut the meat into bite-size pieces. Add the rice to the stock, and bring to a boil. Reduce the heat and return the chicken to the pot. Add the ham pieces. Cover and simmer over low heat until the rice is tender and the water has been absorbed. You may need to stir this once or twice to assure that the rice cooks evenly. Serve the chicken and rice on a large platter garnished with canned french fried onions and sliced hard-boiled eggs.

458 Calories: Fat 18.4 g, Saturated fat 6.2 g, Cholesterol 159 mg, 449 Sodium mg.

Meat Soufflé

3 Tablespoons butter
3 Tablespoons flour
1 cup milk
1 cup cooked chicken or any other cooked meat, minced
2 Tablespoons fresh parsley, chopped
1/2 teaspoon onion powder
2 eggs, separated
cracker crumbs, very finely crushed or Parmesan cheese, grated (if desired)

Because this dish only uses two eggs, it is not as light as a traditional cheese soufflé. This recipe is a different way to use up that last cup of cooked chicken, beef, or fish. Serve with a tomato or mushroom sauce.

It is important to use a perfectly clean bowl and beaters when whipping egg whites. The least bit of grease or egg yolk will prevent them from attaining the proper stiffness.

Yield: 4 servings

Preheat oven to 350°F. Make a white sauce by melting the butter in a medium saucepan. Add the flour and cook until bubbly. Gradually add the milk and cook, stirring constantly, until the sauce is thick. Add the chicken, parsley, and onion powder and set aside to cool slightly. In a medium bowl, beat the egg whites until they form stiff peaks. Combine the egg yolks with the slightly cooled white sauce and then gently fold the mixture into the egg whites. Lightly butter a 7-inch soufflé dish or 1-quart casserole dish with high, straight sides. Dust the butter with cracker crumbs or grated parmesan cheese, if desired. You can also bake this in four individual ramekins. Bake until the soufflé has risen and is firm in the center, about 35 to 40 minutes. Serve immediately.

247 Calories: Fat 14.8 g, Saturated fat 7.8 g, Cholesterol 164 mg, Sodium 189 mg.

Chicken Salad

4 cups cooked chicken, cut into bite-size pieces
2 cups celery, chopped
4 cups cabbage, finely chopped
4 hard-boiled eggs, separated
1/2 cup oil
1 Tablespoon black pepper
2 teaspoons prepared mustard
1 cup vinegar
1/4 cup prepared horseradish, or less
        (not cream-style)

This is a very light salad, almost a cross between chicken salad and coleslaw. Although mayonnaise recipes did appear in Victorian cookbooks, other salad dressings, such as the vinaigrette used here, appear to have been more popular.

Yield: 10 1-cup servings
Combine the chicken and vegetables and set aside in the refrigerator to chill. Mash the egg yolks and combine with the oil, pepper, and mustard. Gradually stir in the vinegar. (You may use the blender or food processor to do this.) Add the horseradish to taste. Just before serving, drain any accumulated juices from the chicken and vegetables and stir in the dressing. Garnish with strips of hard-boiled egg white.

232 Calories: Fat 15 g, Saturated fat 2 g, Cholesterol 131 mg, Sodium 99 mg.

Victoria Chicken

1/3 cup butter
1/2 cup flour
1 1/2 cups chicken stock
1 1/2 cups canned crushed tomatoes
1 teaspoon paprika
2 teaspoons lemon juice
3 cups cooked chicken, cut into bite-size pieces
1 1/2 cups frozen peas

Yield: 6 servings
Melt the butter in a medium saucepan. Add the flour and cook until frothy. Add the stock and tomatoes, and stir until thickened. Add the paprika, lemon juice, chicken, and peas and heat through. Serve in puff pastry cases or over rice.

289 Calories: Fat 13.8 g, Saturated fat 7.3 g, Cholesterol 80 mg, Sodium 643 mg.

Cucumbers in Poulette Sauce

These cucumbers, cooked in a chicken-based sauce, are a mild vegetable side dish that complements the Deviled Chicken (p. 43).

4 large cucumbers
1/4 cup butter or margarine
1/4 cup flour
dash white pepper
2 cups chicken stock
1 Tablespoon lemon juice

Yield: 8 servings

Peel the cucumbers and cut them in half length-wise. Remove the seeds by running a spoon down the center of the cucumber. Cut the cucumbers into 1-inch thick slices. Simmer the slices in water until they are crisp-tender, about 10 minutes. Melt the butter in a medium saucepan. Add the flour and cook until frothy. Add the pepper. Slowly pour in the chicken stock. Cook until thick, and then add the lemon juice and drained cucumber slices. Stir gently and serve.

108 Calories: Fat 8 g, Saturated fat 5 g, Cholesterol 21 mg, Sodium 566 mg.

Deviled Chicken

2 teaspoons dry mustard
1 teaspoon cayenne pepper
3 Tablespoons butter, softened
2 pounds chicken thighs

Keeping the skin on the chicken pieces during baking helps keep the chicken pieces moist, but remove the skins before serving to cut down on calories and fat.

Yield: 15 thighs

Preheat oven to 350°F. Combine the mustard, cayenne pepper, and butter. Wash and wipe the chicken thighs. Gently lift the skin away from the meat, but do not remove it. Make several shallow cuts in the chicken flesh. Rub a little bit of the spiced butter into the chicken meat and pat the skin back down. Bake the chicken until done, about 25 minutes.

125 Calories per piece: Fat 9 g, Saturated fat 3.2 g, Cholesterol 45 mg, Sodium 59 mg.

42

Bread

Like Englishwoman Amelia Murray, most foreign visitors to the United States did not fully appreciate the variety of yeast breads and rolls, biscuits, and corn breads served in American homes and inns. Many of the journals written by European travelers during the nineteenth century decried the lack of good bread here. But, in fact, American bakers took advantage of native grains to make a wide variety of breads. Yeast breads and rolls, as well as quick breads, spoon breads, biscuits, corn breads, and crackers, were made from whole wheat and white flour, mashed potatoes, cornmeal, rice, and oat flours.

Then, as now, good bread was an important part of the daily menu. The Victorian baker frequently began by making her own yeast starter from water in which potatoes had been boiled. This step was critical; many a batch of bread dough had to be discarded because the homemade starter was not strong enough or had become contaminated, yielding loaves which were streaked, soured, and suitable only for feeding to chickens or hogs. By mid-century homemakers could purchase cakes of brewer's or baker's yeast. Still, the Victorian cook was cautioned to check her yeast and flour supplies carefully to avoid adulterated or spoiled products. She might have owned a "patented bread mixer" with an enclosed mixing paddle to help her knead several loaves at a time.

The baking of yeast breads is a time-consuming enterprise involving not only the mixing of the dough, but requiring time for the bread to rise one or two times before baking. To prepare the Lebanon Rolls to serve at afternoon tea, for example, the Victorian baker was instructed to begin by nine in the morning. Although commercially baked breads were available in cities, the conditions under which they were baked, and the quality of the ingredients, were looked upon with suspicion by many homemakers. The careful Victorian homemaker made the baking of bread an important part of her weekly routine.

The earliest quick breads relied on beaten egg whites to help them rise. By the middle of the century, saleratus, a form of baking soda made from potash, was used as a leavening agent in biscuits and other types of breakfast and tea rolls. By the end of the century, commercially packaged baking soda and baking powder were widely available.

I use my large-capacity food processor to mix and knead bread dough and have written the following recipes with those directions. I also use rapid rise active dry yeast. I find, in most instances, it works just as well as regular yeast in far less time. You may certainly make these bread doughs successfully without a food processor. To mix these doughs by hand, combine all of the liquid ingredients in a large mixing bowl. Add half the flour and mix well with a spoon or electric mixer. Then begin adding the remaining flour one cup at a time, mixing by hand only. Once the dough is no longer sticky, turn it out of the bowl onto a clean work surface dusted with flour, and continue kneading in any additional flour necessary to make the dough smooth and elastic. Allow the dough to rise as indicated in the recipes. After making a couple of batches, you will develop a feel for the proper texture of the dough.

Meal served to William Alonzo Hickok (father of "Wild Bill" Hickok)
aboard the Schooner *Virginia Pardee* on July 2, 1851.

Pork and Potatoes

Bread

Fresh Trout

Coffee and Tea

Hickok, William, "Account of a Journey on the Great Lakes,"
Journal of the Illinois State Historical Society, May 1978, p. 144.

Zephyrinas

2 cups flour
2 Tablespoons butter
3/4 cup cold water

Yield: 48 crackers
Preheat oven to 425°F. In the bowl of a food processor fitted with a metal blade, combine the flour and butter. Pulse until well combined and the mixture looks like cornmeal. With the processor running, slowly pour in the cold water and process until the dough forms a ball. Continue processing until the dough is smooth and very pliable. Cover the dough and let it rest for about 15 minutes so that it will be easier to handle. Roll the dough out as thin as possible—the original recipe suggests "as thin as a piece of paper." Cut out with cookie cutters, or slice into squares or diamonds. Sometimes, I find it easier to break off a little piece of dough and roll out each individual cracker, rather than cutting the sheet of dough into shapes. Prick each cracker all over with a fork to keep the dough flat while baking. Place on a lightly greased cookie sheet and bake for 8 to 10 minutes, or until lightly browned.

24 Calories each: Fat .53 g, Saturated fat .30 g, Cholesterol 1.3 mg, Sodium 5 mg.

This 1848 recipe makes a flat, unleavened cracker. The name Zephyrinas probably comes from the Greek root zephyr, meaning light west wind. A bit more substantial than an English water cracker, Zephyrinas are very good keepers. They are a fine foil for a spicy dip such as Deviled Mushrooms (p. 7) or Cheese Mixture for Sandwiches (p. 5).

Nun's Puffs

1 1/4-ounce package rapid rise active dry yeast
1/4 cup warm water
1 cup milk
1 Tablespoon butter
2 Tablespoons sugar
2 eggs
3 cups bread flour

Yield: 24 rolls

Proof the yeast by combining it with the warm water in a large mixing bowl. In the meantime, heat the milk until little bubbles just form around the edge of the pot. Add the butter and sugar and set aside to cool. Combine the eggs with the yeast mixture and beat well. Add the cooled milk mixture. Stir in the flour and mix well. Beat the mixture for 100 strokes with a wooden spoon. Lightly grease two 12-count regular muffin pans and fill them halfway with the soft dough. Set aside in a warm place to rise for about 25 minutes, or until doubled. While puffs are rising, preheat oven to 350°F. Bake for 20 minutes, or until the tops are lightly browned and the rolls sound hollow when tapped. Note: You can also make these rolls in mini muffin pans. Just remember to fill them only halfway up. Your baking time will be somewhat shorter.

80 Calories each: Fat 1.5 g, Saturated fat .68 g, Cholesterol 20 mg, Sodium 12 mg.

For best results mix this bread by hand and make sure you beat it the full 100 strokes.

A-Pees

2 cups flour
1/2 cup sugar
1 teaspoon each ground cinnamon, mace,
    and nutmeg
1/2 cup margarine or butter
1 1/2 Tablespoons caraway seeds
1/3 cup white wine

Yield: 36 crackers
Preheat oven to 375°F. Combine flour, sugar, and spices. Cut in the butter or margarine until the mixture looks like cornmeal. Stir in caraway seeds and wine. Form into a ball and roll the dough out on a lightly floured surface until it is 1/4-inch thick. Cut into shapes. Bake on lightly greased cookie sheets for 15 to 20 minutes, or until just lightly browned. They will still be slightly soft in the center.

64 Calories each: Fat 3 g, Saturated fat .44 g, Cholesterol 0 mg, Sodium 30 mg.

In the Annals of Philadelphia, *J.F. Watson describes A-pees as the product of Ann Page, noted cook, who decorated the crackers with her initials: "A.P." However they were named, A-Pees make a tasty snack with a glass of wine before dinner. Serve them plain or topped with brie. These are better the second day, after the spices have married.*

Sweet Potato Corn Bread

1 cup cooked sweet potato, mashed
1 1/2 cups cornmeal
1 egg
1 Tablespoon butter, softened
1 1/2 cups milk

Yield: 12 servings

Preheat oven to 450°F. Carefully oil a large cast-iron skillet, or individual corn stick molds, and put in the oven to preheat. In a large bowl, combine the mashed sweet potato, cornmeal, egg, and softened butter. Gradually add the milk and mix well. When the pan is hot, but not smoking, carefully pour the batter into them and bake for 10 to 15 minutes, or until the bread has puffed up and set in the center. Let the bread cool slightly and remove from the pan. To bake in pans which are not cast iron, grease individual muffin tins or molds very well and do not preheat them. Put the batter in the cold pans, as you would with any quick bread, and bake for 10 to 15 minutes or until puffed and set.

88 Calories: Fat .16 g, Saturated fat .07 g, Cholesterol 20 mg, Sodium 16 mg.

This is a real pioneer food. It has no leavening agent and is sometimes difficult to cut into nice pieces. If you make it in a large pan, consider serving it as a "spoon bread," dished out of the pan and onto the plates. Try it with some Pineapple Marmalade (p. 12).

Rice and Wheat Bread

1/2 cup uncooked rice
2 cups boiling water
1/2 cup warm water
2 1/4-ounce packages rapid rise active dry yeast
1 Tablespoon honey
5 cups bread flour, or more
1 cup water

Rice and rice flour are found in American cookbooks quite frequently. Here the softly cooked rice adds a lightness and sweetness to the wheat flour bread. The grains of rice will appear lumpy as the bread rises, but the lumps disappear as the bread bakes. This makes really great toast.

Yield: 4 loaves

In a 2-quart pot, combine the 2 cups boiling water and 1/2 cup rice. Cover, lower the heat, and simmer about 20 minutes, or until the water is absorbed and the rice is very soft. Let the rice cool. You can do this step the night before you make the bread. In a measuring cup combine 1/2 cup warm water with the 2 packages of rapid rise yeast and the honey. Set it aside to proof. Once the rice is cool, put it in the bowl of a food processor fitted with a plastic dough blade. Add the flour and begin processing. Pour in the water, honey, and yeast mixture. Continue processing and gradually add 1 more cup water. Do not overprocess this dough. If you process beyond the point at which the dough forms a cohesive ball, the rice will begin to break down and the dough will become wetter and need additional flour. Finish kneading this dough by hand on a floured surface. Set the dough in a lightly greased bowl, turn the dough so the top is greased, cover, and place in a warm place to rise until doubled in bulk. This should take about 1 hour. Punch the dough down and shape it into loaves. Place in greased loaf pans or on baking sheets. Let the dough rise until doubled once again. This should take about 30 minutes. Preheat oven to 350°F while the dough is rising. Bake for 25 to 35 minutes, or until the tops are light brown and the loaves sound hollow when tapped. Remove from pans and cool on their sides on a wire rack.

712 Calories per loaf: Fat 3 g, Saturated fat .45 g, Cholesterol 0 mg, Sodium 4.8 mg.

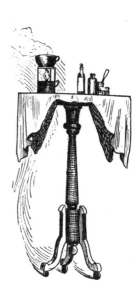

Lebanon Rusk

1/2 cup warm water
1 1/4-ounce package rapid rise active dry yeast
1 cup mashed potato, cooled
1 cup sugar
3 eggs
1/2 cup butter, softened
5 cups bread flour, or more
1 teaspoon ground cinnamon
3 Tablespoons sugar

Leftover mashed potatoes? These tasty rolls are a great (and different) way to use them up. If you don't have leftovers, prepared instant mashed potatoes work just as well.

Yield: 45 rolls

Proof the yeast by combining it with the warm water and setting aside until it begins to foam. In the bowl of a food processor fitted with a plastic dough blade, combine the potatoes, sugar, eggs, and butter. Add the yeast mixture and flour. Process until a smooth ball is formed. You may need to add more flour until the dough is soft and no longer sticky. Put the dough in a lightly oiled bowl, turning it once to oil the top. Cover and let it rise in a warm place until doubled in bulk, about 1 hour. Punch it down and form the dough into small rolls, about 1" x 2". Combine the cinnamon and sugar. Roll the dough in this mixture and set on lightly greased cookie sheets to rise until doubled in bulk, about 30 minutes. Preheat the oven to 350°F while the dough is rising. Bake 15 to 20 minutes, or until lightly brown.

102 Calories each: Fat 2.6 g, Saturated fat 1.4 g, Cholesterol 20 mg, Sodium 26 mg.

Mrs. Kellogg's Whole Wheat Bread

1 1/2 cups warm water
2 1/4-ounce packages rapid rise active dry yeast
2 Tablespoons sugar
4 cups whole wheat flour, divided
4 cups bread flour, divided
1 1/2 cups warm water, additional
1/4 cup molasses

Yield: 4 loaves

Combine the warm water, yeast, and sugar in a large measuring cup. Allow the mixture to stand until it becomes foamy. Put 1 cup of each of the flours in the bowl of a food processor fitted with a plastic dough blade. Add the yeast mixture and process until the batter is smooth. Allow this sponge to rise in the food processor until doubled in bulk. This should take about 15 to 20 minutes. Pulse to deflate the sponge. Add the remaining flour, warm water, and molasses. Process until the dough forms a ball and is smooth. You may have to add a bit more bread flour to assure the dough is not too sticky. Remove from processor and place in a lightly greased bowl. Turn the dough once, so that the surface is greased. Cover and let rise until dough is doubled in bulk, about 1 hour. Punch down and form into four loaves. Place in well-greased loaf pans. Allow to rise until dough is doubled in bulk, about 45 minutes. Preheat the oven to 350°F while the dough is rising. Bake until golden brown and the loaves sound hollow when tapped, about 20 to 30 minutes. Remove from pans and cool the loaves on their sides on racks.

998 Calories per loaf: Fat 4.6 g, Saturated fat .7 g, Cholesterol 0 mg, Sodium 30 mg.

Puddings, Pies, and Ice Creams

"Any pie, to be good, ought to have a light and flaky crust and the filling should be put in sufficiently thick to remove all suspicion of stinginess on the part of the maker."

Dr. A.W. Chase
Dr. Chase's Receipt Book, 1884

Pies are the definitive American dessert. The abundance of fruits and vegetables, coupled with the ease and expediency of preparation, made pie a staple on American tables. Apples, pumpkins, squash, cranberries, and even spaghetti all made their way into Victorian pies. Served at breakfast, lunch, and dinner, carried in a tin pail into the fields or sliced onto a red castle plate in a Philadelphia drawing room, pies were enjoyed by all.

Then as now, the baker's skill set some pies apart from others. Echoing the concerns of Dr. Chase, Mrs. Marion Harland wrote in her *Cookery for Beginners*, "The average pastry of our beloved land would drive a Patrick Henry to self-exile if he were obliged to eat it every day." Many Victorian cookbooks suggested using butter-rich puff pastry as a pie crust. Everyday pie crusts were made with lard. Either crust could turn the best filling into an indigestible concoction. Fortunately, today's cook can use vegetable shortening to make a light and flaky crust.

For the Victorian cook, "pudding" simply meant a baked, steamed, or boiled dessert. We are all familiar with steamed puddings such as Christmas Plum Pudding. Basically a heavy mixture of suet, raisins, flour, and other spices, steamed puddings take a long time to cook on top of the stove. Despite their dominance in Victorian cookery, I have elected not to include any steamed or boiled puddings in this volume. They are more British than American and they are, frankly, a lot of bother to make. I have included a Baked Carrot Pudding which has a flavor and texture similar to that of boiled pudding. Some of the other desserts called puddings here fall into the general category of pudding as a synonym for sweet.

Ice creams and frozen desserts were especially popular in the mid- to late-Victorian era both in the United States and in England. Then as now, vanilla and fruit flavors were popular. The recipes for Tutti-Frutti and Brown Ice Creams demonstrate some of the other rich and dense flavors popular during this period.

53

Apple Custard Pudding

4 cups tart apples, peeled and sliced
1/2 cup water
1 lemon
1/2 cup sugar
2 Tablespoons butter
2 Tablespoons flour
1/2 teaspoon ground nutmeg
1 teaspoon ground cinnamon
2 cups dry bread crumbs
2 eggs

Yield: 12 servings

Preheat oven to 325°F. Put the apples and water into a heavy saucepan. Cook until soft. While the apples are cooking, juice the lemon and grate the rind. Remove from heat and add the sugar, butter, grated lemon rind, and lemon juice. Mash the apples until they are the consistency of applesauce. Mix the flour, nutmeg, and cinnamon with bread crumbs and stir this mixture into the apple mixture. Separate the eggs. Add the yolks to the apple mixture. Beat the egg whites in a clean bowl with grease-free beaters until they form soft peaks. Gently fold them into the apple mixture. Turn into a buttered 9" x 12" pan. Bake for 30 to 40 minutes, or until set through. Serve with Wine Sauce (p.55) or ice cream.

159 Calories: Fat 3.7 g, Saturated fat 1.7 g, Cholesterol 41 mg, Sodium 153 mg.

Wine Sauce

1 cup butter
2 cups sifted confectioners' sugar
1 dash nutmeg
1/2 cup sherry

Yield: 3 cups

Beat the butter until smooth. Mix confectioners' sugar with nutmeg, and gradually add the mixture to the butter. Beat in the sherry, one Tablespoon at a time, until it is completely incorporated. Store sauce in a covered container in the refrigerator until ready to serve. Put a dollop on hot puddings, cakes, or pies.

77 Calories per Tablespoon: Fat 5 g, Saturated fat 3 g, Cholesterol 13.8 mg, Sodium 52 mg.

Lemon Sauce for Sweet Puddings

1 lemon
1 Tablespoon butter
1 Tablespoon flour
1 cup sherry
1 cup water
4 egg yolks
1/2 cup sugar

Yield: 2 1/2 cups

Grate the rind from the lemon and squeeze out the juice. Combine the butter and flour in a saucepan and stir over medium heat until the mixture is light brown. Add the sherry, water, lemon juice, and lemon rind. Cook, stirring constantly, until the sauce is slightly thickened. Lightly beat the egg yolks and the sugar in a heatproof container. Add a little of the hot lemon and wine sauce to the egg mixture. When the egg mixture is warmed by the addition of this sauce, add the remaining sauce. Cook over low heat, stirring constantly, until the sauce thickens. Do not allow it to boil, or the egg yolks will curdle. Serve with any plain cake or over a fruit shortcake.

36 Calories per Tablespoon: Fat .8 g, Saturated fat .4 g, Cholesterol 28 mg, Sodium 5.6 mg.

Date Pie

1 8-ounce package pitted dates
1 1/2 cups milk
1 egg
1/2 teaspoon ground cinnamon
8-inch packaged graham cracker pie crust
      (or individual tart crusts)

This is a very rich pie. A small slice goes a long way and is nicely complemented by the Brown Ice Cream (p. 59). Make sure you use an 8-inch prepared pie crust.

Yield: 8 servings

Preheat oven to 350°F. Combine the pitted dates and the milk in a small saucepan. Cook over low heat until the dates are soft. Process in a blender or food processor until smooth. Add the egg and cinnamon. Carefully pour the date mixture in the graham cracker pie crust. It will appear very runny. Bake for 50 to 60 minutes, or until filling is completely set.

473 Calories: Fat 11 g, Saturated fat 6.9 g, Cholesterol 53.1 mg, Sodium 280 mg.

There are three keys to making a flaky pie crust. First, make sure the cold fat is well cut into the flour. Use a wire pastry cutter, or quickly pulse the mixture in a food processor so that very small particles of fat are coated with flour. Second, use ice-cold water to bind the dough. Third, handle the dough as little as possible so that the heat from your hands does not melt the fat in the dough before it is baked.

Basic Pie Crust

3 cups flour
1 1/2 cups margarine
1/2 cup ice-cold water

Yield: pastry for two 9-inch, 2-crust pies plus an extra bottom crust.

Cut the fat into the flour with a pastry cutter, two knives, or a food processor until the mixture looks like cornmeal. Add the cold water slowly and mix with a fork, until it just holds together in a ball. Chill and roll the pastry out on a floured surface to fit your pie plate.

4,100 Calories whole recipe: Fat 311 g, Saturated fat 121 g, Cholesterol 292 mg, Sodium 7.5 mg.

The original yield for this recipe stated it was enough for four pies, but Victorian pie plates tended to be smaller than the ones we use today. Take this into consideration if you adapt any historical pie recipes.

Victorian pie crust recipes called for lard, or half lard and half butter. I use 100 percent margarine. The resulting crust may not be quite as flaky and the flavor is not as rich, but it is much healthier.

Ingredients for Another Basic Pie Crust

1 cup flour
1/4 teaspoon baking powder
1/2 cup margarine
3 Tablespoons ice-cold water

Yield: Pastry for one 8-inch, 2-crust pie or one bottom crust for a larger pie.

Combine the flour and baking powder. Add margarine and water as above.

1,279 Calories whole recipe: Fat 93 g, Saturated fat 58 g, Cholesterol 248 mg, Sodium 1,029 mg.

Combination Pie

10-inch bottom pie crust
3 cups cranberries
2 cups sugar
2 Tablespoons flour
2 eggs, separated
1/2 cup sugar
1/2 cup flour
1 teaspoon water
1 teaspoon baking powder

This is the perfect holiday dessert when you can't decide between cake and pie. The tart cranberry filling is topped off with a very light sponge cake.

Yield: 10 servings

Preheat oven to 350°F. Line a 10-inch pie plate with your favorite pie crust. Wash and pick over the cranberries. Blot dry. Combine the cranberries, sugar, and flour in a food processor fitted with a metal blade. Pulse three or four times, until the cranberries are slightly chopped. Let them stand for a couple of minutes and stir to begin dissolving the sugar. Pour this mixture into the pie crust. Bake until filling is done, about 30 minutes. While the pie is baking, prepare the sponge cake batter. Separate the eggs. Using grease-free beaters and a clean bowl, beat the egg whites until stiff and set aside. Combine the egg yolks with the sugar and beat until fluffy. Add the flour, water, and baking powder to the egg yolk mixture. Fold the egg whites into this batter, and pour over the top of the baked pie. Return to the oven and bake another 20 minutes, or until the sponge cake is firm and lightly browned.

Note: The cranberry filling will not come up to the top of the pie crust. As it bakes, watch to make sure the unfilled portion of the pie crust does not collapse into the filling. I have had to open the oven and push the pie crust back over the rim of the pie pan on some occasions.

360 Calories: Fat 8.8 g, Saturated fat 3.3 g, Cholesterol 50.3 mg, Sodium 49 mg.

Brown Ice Cream

Ice and hand-cranked ice cream freezers were readily available throughout the Victorian era. Ice cream was a popular treat, with vanilla, strawberry, and other fruit flavors made with recipes just like those we use today. The selected recipes here highlight some of the more exotic flavors developed during the period.

2 cups skim milk
3 cups light brown sugar, firmly packed
3 12-ounce cans evaporated skim milk

Yield: 2 quarts

In a medium saucepan, combine the skim milk and brown sugar. Cook, stirring frequently, until the sugar is dissolved and the syrup is thickened, about 20 minutes. Chill in the freezer compartment of your refrigerator until ice just begins to form around the edges. Combine the brown sugar mixture with the evaporated skim milk. Put into an ice cream freezer and process according to directions.

184 Calories per 1/2 cup: Fat .2 g, Saturated fat .1 g, Cholesterol 3.2 mg, Sodium 1.1 mg.

I have made these highly flavored ice creams with low-fat milk products rather than cream. Of course, you could substitute equal measures of half-and-half or whipping cream, but I don't think that's necessary.

Tutti-Frutti Ice Cream

1/4 cup currants
1/4 cup sherry
2 cups low-fat milk
2 egg yolks
3 cups sugar
4 cups cream or nonfat evaporated milk
1 lemon
4 ounces mixed candied fruits

Yield: 2 quarts

Heat the currants in the sherry to plump them and set aside. Make a custard by combining the milk, sugar, and egg yolks in a medium saucepan. Cook over medium heat, stirring, until thickened enough to coat the back of a spoon. Remove from the heat and cool, first to room temperature, then in the freezer compartment of your refrigerator until ice crystals just begin to form. Mix well with the cream, or evaporated milk. Process in an ice cream freezer until halfway frozen. Grate the peel from the lemon and juice it. Then add the lemon juice and peel, candied fruits, currants, and wine to the ice cream and mix thoroughly. Continue processing until firm.

234 Calories per 1/2 cup: Fat 11 g, Saturated fat 6.7 g, Cholesterol 54 mg, Sodium 26 mg.

When processing ice creams, use between 3 to 6 measures of ice to 1 of salt. The more salt you use, the faster the ice cream will freeze. The slower it freezes, the smoother it will be. I have also found it helpful to chill the mixture in the refrigerator or freezer before processing it in the ice cream freezer. I have both a hand-cranked and an electric ice cream freezer. Ice cream freezers are relatively simple pieces of kitchen equipment. If you are thinking of purchasing one, I would suggest picking one with the largest capacity you can. I've found the more I make fresh ice cream, the more my family likes to eat it. There is never enough!

Vermicelli Pudding

4 ounces vermicelli
3 cups milk
1 cup half-and-half
3 Tablespoons butter
1/3 cup sugar
3 eggs
1 teaspoon vanilla
1/6 of a 17 1/2-ounce package of frozen puff pastry
(see note)

Yield: 10 servings
Preheat the oven to 350°F. Break the pasta up into 1-inch pieces. Combine the vermicelli with the milk, bring to a boil, then lower the heat and simmer until pasta is very tender. Cool slightly, then stir in the remaining ingredients, except the puff pastry. Butter a 10-inch pie plate and line only the sides with puff pastry. Pour in the pudding filling and bake for 45 minutes, or until it is firmly set in the middle.

198 Calories: Fat 10.3 g, Saturated fat 6 g, Cholesterol 92 mg, Sodium 100 mg.

Pasta for dessert? In this late-Victorian recipe, pasta is cooked in milk and sugar. The resulting texture is similar to that of rice pudding. The puff pastry around the pie plate provides an elegant crust.

Note: I use 17 1/2-ounce packaged frozen puff pastry which is packaged two sheets per box. For this recipe you only need one-third of one of the sheets.

Baked Carrot Pudding

12 ounces carrots
8 ounces bread crumbs
1/4 cup butter
4 ounces raisins
4 ounces currants
1/2 cup sugar
3 eggs
1/4 cup milk
1/4 teaspoon nutmeg
confectioners' sugar for topping

Yield: 12 servings

Preheat the oven to 350°F. Scrape the carrots and slice them. Boil until tender, drain and mash into a pulp. Combine with the remaining ingredients except the confectioners' sugar. Pour into a lightly greased baking dish, and set the dish in a larger pan filled with an inch of boiling water. Bake for 1 hour or until set in the center. Sprinkle with sifted confectioners' sugar and serve with Wine Sauce (p. 55).

213 Calories: Fat 6.2 g, Saturated fat 3 g, Cholesterol 65 mg, Sodium 207 mg.

This dense carrot dessert is similar in flavor and texture to a traditional Victorian steamed pudding. Puddings such as this would have been cooked by putting the batter in a canvas or heavy muslin cloth, which was then tied up tightly and placed in a large kettle of boiling water. These puddings required several hours boiling to cook through. Later, decorative metal or ceramic pudding molds were used in place of the cloth, but the steaming process still took hours.

Cakes and Cookies

"There is as much in putting cakes together as in the proportion."

Mrs. E.F. Haskell
Housekeepers Encyclopedia, 1869

Once, simply knowing the list of ingredients was enough for a home-maker to prepare a satisfactory cake for her family. As you can see from the recipe for Tennessee Cake, early Victorian cakes were only slightly sweet and more breadlike. The introduction of chemical leavening agents enabled bakers to incorporate rich ingredients and produce a wide assortment of fluffy, buttery, and light-textured desserts. For example, with the addition of baking soda and sour milk, gingerbread was elevated from a flat, slightly crisp cookie into the light cake we enjoy today.

In a uniquely American practice, cakes were named for national heroes, events, and places. Victorian cooks prepared Washington Cake, as well as cakes named for General Robert E. Lee and presidential candidate Samuel Tilden. Victorian hostesses could make a political statement just by serving dessert. Just imagine the conversation that might have taken place over a dessert of Southern Rights and Lincoln Cakes! The flavors of these Victorian cakes were as varied as their names. Fresh and candied fruits, spices, and the rich sweetness of brown sugar and molasses give these cakes an assertiveness not found in today's basic yellow, white, and chocolate cakes.

Nineteenth century cooking equipment also improved the process of cake and cookie baking. The Dover Beater, the first geared wire egg beater, helped the cook whip up egg whites. The enclosed firebox of the new stoves provided a more even heat surrounding the baking cake. However, great skill was required to build and bank the fire, adjust the dampers of the stove, and judge the proper temperature. The 1877 *Buckeye Cookery and Practical House-keeper* dedicates half a page to these skills, concluding, "If the hand can be held in from twenty-five to thirty seconds it is a 'quick' oven, from thirty-five to forty is 'moderate' and from forty-five to sixty is 'slow'."

By the end of the century baking powder, either purchased or made by the homemaker from baking soda and cream of tartar, was commonly used as a leavening agent. Although there was a great deal of discussion about the reliability and purity of both baking powder and baking soda, many late-Victorian recipes called for their use without hesitation. The original instructions to dissolve these rising agents may not be necessary with today's finely milled products, but I have retained those directions anyway. Both soda and baking powder begin to act when they are wet, so to best simulate the Victorian leavening agents and the resulting cake texture, mix as indicated.

Mrs. Kellogg's Picnic Lunch

Carrot Soup

Graham Bread

Fruit Sandwiches

Egg Sandwiches

Fig Wafers

Seasonable Fruit

Orange Cake

Raspberry Shrub

Milk

Lemonade

Mrs. Kellogg suggested picnic foods be as simple as possible and not of too great a variety. In keeping with the healthful, almost vegetarian, regimen served at the Kellogg Sanitarium in Battle Creek, Michigan, this is her recommendation for a suitable picnic.

Kellogg, E.E. *Science in the Kitchen*. Battle Creek, MI: Health Publishing Company Battle Creek Michigan, 1892.

Tennessee Cake

4 eggs, separated
1/4 cup butter
1/2 cup brown sugar, firmly packed
1/2 cup flour
1 cup cornmeal
1 teaspoon ground cinnamon
1 1/4 teaspoons ground nutmeg

This early Victorian recipe, made from pioneer and American ingredients, has no leavening agent other than the well-beaten egg whites. Serve with Vinegar Sauce (below) or Lemon Sauce (p. 55). Although this is not a rich cake, a small serving is plenty.

Yield: 14 servings

Preheat oven to 350°F. Using grease-free beaters and a clean bowl, beat the egg whites until stiff and set aside. Cream the butter and brown sugar. Add the egg yolks and mix well. Combine the flour, cornmeal, and spices and add to the batter. Gently fold in the beaten egg whites. Pour batter into a greased and floured 7" x 11" pan. Bake for 30 minutes, or until a toothpick inserted in the center comes out clean.

174 Calories: Fat 9.6 g, Saturated fat 5.4 g, Cholesterol 92 mg, Sodium 100 mg.

Vinegar Sauce

1 1/2 cups sugar
1 1/2 Tablespoons flour
3 cups water
2 Tablespoons vinegar
2 Tablespoons butter
1/2 teaspoon ground nutmeg

Yield: 4 cups

Combine the sugar and flour. Slowly add the water, stirring constantly with a wire whisk. Bring to a boil and cook over medium heat for 10 minutes. Stir in the vinegar, butter, and nutmeg. Serve with gingerbread, plain cake, or Tennessee Cake (p. 65).

30 Calories per Tablespoon: Fat .49 g, Saturated fat .03 g, Cholesterol 1.3 mg, Sodium 5 mg.

Cherry Wine Sauce

1 package frozen unsweetened cherries
2 cups white wine
1 cup sugar

Yield: 2 cups

Process the cherries in a food processor or blender. Mix with the wine and sugar. Cook over medium heat in a large, heavy saucepan until the mixture is the consistency of heavy cream. You really need to watch this as it cooks and stir it occasionally. In the beginning it has a tendency to bubble up and over the sides, and at the end, as it thickens, it may stick and scorch. Serve with the Tilden Cake (p.69) or ice cream.

42 Calories per Tablespoon: Fat .02 g, Saturated fat 0 g, Cholesterol 0 mg, Sodium 1 mg.

Washington Cake

9 ounces currants
1 cup sherry or any other wine, divided
3/4 cup butter
1 1/2 cups sugar
3 large eggs
3 cups flour, sifted
1 1/2 teaspoons ground cinnamon
1 1/2 teaspoons ground nutmeg
3/4 teaspoon baking soda
1 cup light cream

This simple cake, named for the father of our country, is a tasty combination of fruit, spices, and wine. Washington Cake is a nice change from cherry pie on February 22.

Yield: 24 servings

Preheat oven to 350°F. Heat the currants in a small bowl or pan with 1/2 cup sherry and set aside to plump. Cream the butter and sugar. Add the eggs and mix well. Sift the flour with the spices and add to the mixture. Add the remaining 1/2 cup sherry. Dissolve the baking soda in the cream and add to the batter. Finally, stir in the currants. Pour the batter into a greased and floured tube or bundt pan and bake for 1 hour, or until top is lightly browned and the cake is just pulling away from the sides. Cool for 10 minutes in the pan, and finish cooling on a cake rack.

250 Calories: Fat 15 g, Saturated fat 9.3 g, Cholesterol 69 mg, Sodium 147 mg.

Lincoln Cake

3 1/2 cups flour
1 teaspoon baking soda
1/2 teaspoon ground nutmeg
1/2 teaspoon ground cloves
1 1/2 teaspoons ground cinnamon
8 ounces raisins
4 ounces currants
2 ounces candied citrus peel
4 ounces almonds
1/2 cup flour, for dredging the fruits
1 cup butter
1 1/2 cups brown sugar, firmly packed
3 eggs, beaten
1 cup milk
1/4 cup brandy

This is a very nice, light fruitcake. If you wrap it well in plastic wrap and seal it in a tin or plastic bag, it keeps for months in the refrigerator. Take it out once a month or so, and baste it with a little brandy to keep it moist.

Yield: 24 servings

Preheat oven to 325°F. Mix 3 1/2 cups flour, baking soda, and spices and set aside. Mix the dried fruits, citrus peel, and nuts with 1/2 cup flour and set aside. Cream the butter and brown sugar. Add the eggs and mix well. Add the flour and spice mixture alternately with first the milk and then the brandy, beginning and ending with flour mixture. Stir in the flour, fruit, and nut mixture. Pour mixture into a well-greased and floured pan. The batter makes one large tube or bundt cake and one loaf cake. Bake for approximately 1 hour, or until a toothpick stuck in the center comes out clean.

293 Calories per slice: Fat 11.4 g, Saturated fat 5.5 g, Cholesterol 49 mg, Sodium 132 mg.

68

Tilden Cake

This cake is named for Samuel Tilden, an attorney who was responsible for successfully prosecuting Boss Tweed and who later served as governor of New York. Tilden was the Democratic nominee for president of the United States in 1876. He won the popular election, beating Rutherford B. Hayes by more than a quarter of a million votes. However, he did not have a majority of the electoral college votes. Tilden carried the southern states; Hayes, the northern. Four states had disputed returns. In the end, Hayes was elected by the Congressional Compromise of 1877, and Tilden had a cake named after him.

4 eggs, separated
1 cup butter
1 cup sugar
2 teaspoons lemon extract
2 1/2 cups flour
1/2 cup cornstarch
2 teaspoons baking powder
1 cup milk

Yield: 12 servings

Preheat oven to 350°F. In a medium-size bowl, beat the egg whites with grease-free beaters until soft peaks form. Set aside. In a large bowl, cream the butter and sugar until fluffy. Add the egg yolks and mix well. Stir in the lemon extract. Sift the flour, cornstarch, and baking powder together. Add this mixture alternately with the milk in three additions, beginning and ending with the flour mixture. Gently fold in the beaten egg whites. Pour batter into a greased and floured bundt or tube pan. Bake for 45 minutes, or until a toothpick stuck in the center comes out clean. Cool in the pan for 10 minutes, then cool completely on a cake rack.

355 Calories: Fat 18 g, Saturated fat 11 g, Cholesterol 115 mg, Sodium 247 mg.

Southern Rights Cake

3 eggs, separated
1 cup sugar
1 cup butter
1/2 cup molasses
2 cups flour
1 1/2 Tablespoons ground cinnamon
1 1/2 Tablespoons ground ginger
1 1/2 Tablespoons ground allspice
1/2 teaspoon baking powder
1/2 cup bourbon

Yield: 60 servings
Preheat oven to 350°F. In a small bowl and using
clean beaters, beat the egg whites until they form
soft peaks and set aside. Cream the butter and sugar,
add the egg yolks, and mix until lemon-colored. Stir
in the molasses and mix well. Sift the dry ingredients together and add alternately with the bourbon.
Gently fold in the egg whites. Pour batter into five
well-greased and floured 5" x 3" loaf pans. Bake 35
to 45 minutes, or until firm and just beginning to
pull away from the sides of the pans. Frost with white
confectioners' sugar icing.

60 Calories per serving: Fat 3.3 g, Saturated fat 2 g, Cholesterol .19 g,
Sodium 40 mg.

*I found
Southern Rights Cake
in the Dixie Cookbook,
published in 1865.
My feeling is that this rich
gingerbread was named
during the dark days of the
civil war. Whatever the
reason for the name, this is a
wonderful cake. You can
make a terrific ice cream
sandwich by layering Brown
Ice Cream (p. 59) between
two chilled slices of Southern
Rights Cake and returing to
the freezer until firm.*

70

Brown Spice Cake

1/4 cup butter
1/2 cup brown sugar, firmly packed
2 eggs
1/3 cup molasses
1/2 cup flour
1/4 cup dry cocoa
1/2 teaspoon baking soda
1 teaspoon baking powder
1 teaspoon ground cinnamon
1 teaspoon ground mace
1/2 teaspoon ground nutmeg
1/4 teaspoon ground cloves
1/2 cup black coffee, brewed strong
1/2 cup chopped walnuts (optional)

Dutch-processed powdered chocolate was available throughout the nineteenth century, but it was very expensive. In Victorian cookbooks, chocolate was most often used as a filling or as part of the mix of flavoring ingredients, rather than as the primary flavoring ingredient. Chocolate and devil's food cakes became popular in the 1920s and 1930s.

Yield: 9 servings

Preheat oven to 325°F. Cream the butter and sugar. Add the eggs and mix until light and lemon-colored. Add the molasses and mix well. Sift the flour and other dry ingredients. Add the dry ingredients alternately with the coffee, beginning and ending with the dry ingredients. Stir in the nuts, if desired. Bake in a greased and floured 9-inch square pan 30 to 35 minutes, or until the cake is firm and just pulls away from the sides of the pan.

193 Calories: Fat 6.6 g, Saturated fat 3.6 g, Cholesterol 61 mg, Sodium 165 mg.

Mrs F.'s Soft Gingerbread

3 eggs

1 cup butter

2 cups dark brown sugar, firmly packed

1 teaspoon cinnamon

1 Tablespoon ginger

4 cups flour

1 cup milk, soured with 2 Tablespoons vinegar or
        lemon juice

1 teaspoon baking soda

1/4 cup hot water

Yield: 84 squares

Preheat oven to 375°F. Separate the eggs. Using clean beaters, beat the egg whites in a grease-free bowl until they form stiff peaks. Set aside. Cream the butter and brown sugar together. Add the egg yolks and mix thoroughly. Add the cinnamon and ginger. Add 2 cups of the flour and combine well. Add the soured milk and mix, then add the remaining flour. Dissolve the baking soda in the hot water and add the mixture to the batter. Carefully fold in the beaten egg whites. Grease and flour two 15" x 12" x 1" jelly roll pans. Pat the dough into place. Bake for 20 minutes or until lightly browned and firm. Cut into squares and store in a covered container.

57 Calories each: Fat 2.5 g, Saturated fat 1.5 g, Cholesterol 14 mg, Sodium 36.8 mg.

Ginger in its various forms was used as a digestive aid. I have read letters from a Confederate soldier asking to have ginger sent from home to counteract the effects of military rations. This gingerbread from an 1865 cookbook uses baking soda and sour milk to make a lighter bar than the crisp, more cookie-like gingerbreads which were popular in the colonial period.

Mrs. Jemison's Jumbles

*Jumbles are one of the
earliest types of cookies.
This jumble recipe is
from the handwritten 1862
household book of
Mrs. Robert Jemison,
wife of a wealthy
Tuscaloosa, Alabama,
planter. Her husband
served in the Alabama
State Senate and, later, in
the senate of the Confederacy
from 1863 through 1865.
During the Civil War,
Mrs. Jemison may have sent
a tin of these cookies along
with the senator as he
journeyed back to the capital
of the Confederacy in
Richmond, Virginia.*

1 cup butter
1 cup sugar
2 eggs
4 cups flour, sifted before measuring
1 teaspoon mace
1 teaspoon baking soda
1/3 cup sugar

Yield: 8 dozen jumbles

Preheat oven to 350°F. Cream the butter and sugar. Add the eggs and mix well. Sift the flour with the baking soda and mace, and combine with other ingredients. Traditionally these cookies are formed in a flat "doughnut" shape. You can either roll them out on a floured surface and cut them with cookie cutters, or form them by hand, as I prefer to do. To make the cookies by hand, break off a piece of dough the size of a tennis ball and place it on a large flat surface. Gently roll the dough under your palms, forming a long sausage shape. Continue rolling, gradually making this tube longer and thinner. When it is about 12 inches long, break it in half. Roll this half until it is the diameter of a pencil. Break the dough into sections about 3 inches in length. Gently taper the ends and join them in a ring, pressing them together firmly. Flatten the cookie slightly, dip the top side into the granulated sugar, and place on a greased cookie sheet, leaving an inch or so between the cookies. Bake for 10 to 12 minutes, or until just lightly browned.

45 Calories each: Fat 2 g, Saturated fat 1 g, Cholesterol .1 g, Sodium 30 mg.

New Year's Cookies

2 cups sugar
3/4 cup butter or margarine
3 eggs, lightly beaten
3 cups flour
1 teaspoon baking soda
1/2 cup milk
1/2 teaspoon cream of tartar
1/4 cup warm water
1 teaspoon ground cardamom
3 Tablespoons caraway seeds

Yield: 8 dozen

Preheat oven to 375°F. Cream the butter and sugar, add the eggs, and mix well. Stir in 1 cup of the flour and mix well. Dissolve the baking soda in the milk and add to the mixture. Add 1 more cup of flour and mix well. Dissolve the cream of tartar in the warm water and add to the mixture. Stir in the remaining cup of flour with the cardamom and caraway seeds. Chill the dough until firm. Drop by half teaspoons onto lightly greased sheets. Press flat with the bottom of a flat-bottomed glass dipped in granulated sugar. Bake for 10 minutes, or until cookies are lightly brown around the edges. Remove to baking rack and cool.

60 Calories each: Fat 3 g, Saturated fat 1.8 g, Cholesterol 14.6 mg, Sodium 41 mg.

The word cookie comes from the Dutch koekje, meaning "little cakes." In colonial New York, koekjes were offered to New Year's visitors. These Victorian New Year's Cookies are an example of the inclusion of savory spices and seeds in a sweet treat. Cardamom and caraway seeds — unusual flavors for a cookie — make eating these treats a very interesting way to kick off the New Year.

74

Mrs. Kellogg's Fig Wafers

1 8-ounce package dried figs
1 1/2 cups whole wheat flour
6-8 Tablespoons half-and-half

Yield: 48 wafers

Preheat oven to 350°F. In the bowl of a food processor combine the figs and flour. Process until the mixture looks like cornmeal. With the processor running, slowly add the half-and-half until you can form a soft ball of dough. Roll the dough out very thin on a lightly floured surface. Cut into shapes with a cookie cutter. Put on lightly greased baking sheets. Bake 15 to 20 minutes, or until lightly browned around the edges. Cool on rack.

80 Calories each: Fat 9.6 g, Saturated fat 5.4 g, Cholesterol 92 mg, Sodium 100 mg.

Walnut Molasses Bars

1/2 cup butter
1/2 cup brown sugar, firmly packed
1/4 cup boiling water
1/2 cup molasses
1 teaspoon baking soda
3 cups flour
1/2 teaspoon ground ginger
1/4 teaspoon ground nutmeg
dash ground cloves
1 egg white
1 Tablespoon water
3/4 cup walnuts, finely chopped
1/4 cup sugar

These crisp cookies have a mild, gingery flavor. They are good keepers, if you have any left over to keep!

Yield: 8 dozen bars
Preheat oven to 350°F. Cream the butter and brown sugar. Stir in the molasses, baking soda, and boiling water. Mix in the dry ingredients. Chill the dough until it can be handled easily, about 1 hour. Roll out to 1/4-inch thick on a lightly floured surface. Cut into 1-inch squares. Place on greased cookie sheets. Combine water and egg white and brush tops of cookies with this mixture. Combine walnuts and sugar and sprinkle over tops of cookies, pressing the topping gently to help it stick to the unbaked cookie. Bake 10 to 15 minutes, or until lightly browned.

34 Calories each: Fat 1.5 g, Saturated fat .65 g, Cholesterol 2.6 mg, Sodium 19.4 mg.

Kelley Island Cake

1 cup butter
2 cups sugar
4 eggs
3 cups flour
1 Tablespoon baking powder
1/2 cup milk
confectioners' sugar
2 lemons
2 large, tart apples
2 eggs
2 cups sugar

Yield: 24 servings

Preheat oven to 350°F. Cream the butter and sugar. Add 4 eggs and mix well. Combine the flour and baking powder, and add to the batter alternately with the milk, beginning and ending with the flour mixture. Spread the batter in two greased and floured jelly roll pans, lined with waxed or parchment paper. Bake until just set, about 15 to 20 minutes. When the cake is done, sift confectioners' sugar over the top, and place a clean, lint-free linen or cotton dish towel on top of it. Turn the pan over to release the cake. Peel the paper off the back of the cake, dust with confectioners' sugar, and cover with a second towel. Immediately roll the cake up from the narrow end, rolling the cloths inside the cake. Allow to cool while you prepare the filling. Grate the peel from the lemons and extract the juice. Peel and dice the apple into small pieces. Combine apples, lemon peel, lemon juice, eggs, and sugar in a medium saucepan and cook over low heat until the sauce is clear and thick and the apples are tender. To fill the cake, gently unroll the cake and towels. Remove the top towel and spread the slightly cooled filling on the cake. Reroll the cake, using the bottom towel to lift the cake around the filling to make a tight roll. If the cake cracks during this unrolling and rolling process, don't worry, the filling will make it stick together. Wrap in plastic wrap or foil and refrigerate until served.

372 Calories: Fat 10 g, Saturated fat 5 g, Cholesterol 92 mg, Sodium 145 mg.

Kelley Island lies in Lake Erie, just off the shore near Toledo, Ohio. Its northern shore is on the international boundary between the United States and Canada. Purchased by the Kelley brothers in 1833, the island served as a summer resort beginning in the 1870s. It is said that many travelers visited this rustic island. Perhaps one of them was moved to create this cake in memory of summer days spent watching the steamboats running between Sandusky and Detroit.